WHEREVER I FIND MYSELF

Caitlin Press Inc.
8100 Alderwood Road, Halfmoon Bay, BC V0N 1Y1
www.caitlin-press.com

Text and cover design by Vici Johnstone
Cover image Christopher Sardegna (chrissardegna.com)
Image on page 5-6 Jayakumar Ananthan (unsplash.com/@jk)

Printed in Canada

Caitlin Press Inc. acknowledges financial support from the Government of
Canada and the Canada Council for the Arts, and the Province of British
Columbia through the British Columbia Arts Council and the Book Pub-
lisher's Tax Credit.

Library and Archives Canada Cataloguing in Publication

Wherever I find myself : stories by Canadian immigrant
    women / edited by Miriam Matejova.

    ISBN 978-1-987915-34-1 (softcover)

    1. Women immigrants—Canada—Anecdotes. 2. Women
    immigrants—Canada—Social conditions—Anecdotes.
    I. Matejova, Miriam, editor

JV7284.W44 2017   305.48'4120971   C2016-907711-X

WHEREVER
I FIND *myself*

STORIES BY CANADIAN IMMIGRANT WOMEN

EDITED BY

MIRIAM MATEJOVA

CAITLIN PRESS

To the restless, the lonely, and those
forever stuck in between.

Contents

I long, as does every human being, to be at home wherever I find myself.

—Maya Angelou

Introduction

MIRIAM MATEJOVA

As I sit down to write an introduction to this anthology, immigrants from selected countries are being denied entry into the United States. Anti-immigrant attitudes are on the rise in Europe. In the Western world, the far right is clashing with the far left, with immigrants often caught in the middle. Hateful rhetoric and acts of vandalism are aimed at people who are perceived as outsiders, as not belonging, as threatening.

I am an immigrant. I came from Slovakia as an eighteen-year-old, wishing to study at a Canadian university. Back then I was an outsider. I did not belong. But far from threatening, I was lonely, clueless and utterly terrified.

At first I lived with my estranged father, a man whom I knew mostly from flashes of childhood memories and stories my grandmother used to tell with reprehension she didn't care to hide. Living with him turned me into a young woman with downcast eyes, a trembling voice and recurrent nail marks in the palms of my hands. Seven months later I found myself standing on his doorstep, waiting for a taxi to take me to a women's shelter. As I saw the car approaching, I lifted my chin and promised myself: My back would never again be pinned against the wall, with my feet dangling in the air and my throat being squeezed in intervals harmonized with the rhythm of angry curses. From then on I would add volume to my voice. I would leave no nail marks in the palms of my hands.

Without the kindness and help that I received from strangers—
from Canadians I met in the coming years—I never would have been
able to keep those promises. My English was broken and my knowledge of Canadian customs minimal. I owned two bags of clothes,
three pairs of shoes, a chipped Walkman, a handful of cassette tapes
and three books: a Slovak–English dictionary, the Dalai Lama's *The
Art of Happiness*, and a book of collected ghost stories. I had twenty dollars in cash and a few thousand in a student loan that ran out
before my first year at the university was over. I was lonely, wilfully
hopeful of my future and constantly afraid that my old country had
forgotten me while my new one refused to fully accept me. Yet my
first years in Canada were filled with experiences I have never regretted: (some) failed relationships and lasting friendships, the first time
I drank beer and the time I tried learning how to snowboard by myself, those two months when I lived on about thirty dollars per month
worth of groceries, and the seeds of my love affair with coffee and
Tim Hortons' Boston creams.

Over the years snippets of experiences have accumulated in my
desk drawers, written on scraps of paper, yellow folder dividers, neon
Post-it Notes and airplane napkins. Although I have always wanted
to write about my beginnings in Canada, I have not yet put these
pieces together. I haven't been able to find a common theme or one
particular experience to focus on. There have been too many.

This anthology accomplishes what I have not yet been able to.
While they don't speak for all, together the authors of these stories
reveal what it means to be a Canadian immigrant woman. They move
around restlessly, unable to find a place to convincingly call home.
They learn a new language, give up parts of their identities (and ac-
quire new ones) and adjust their expectations. Some search for their
origins. Others try to understand their parents, first-generation immigrants. They learn how to explain who they are and where they
came from as well as how to tell strangers when to stop asking. They
often encounter misunderstanding, hostility, racism or ignorance.
They cling to aspects of their old homes while attempting to blend
into a new society, only to remain somewhere in between. Their stories are about determination, faith, sacrifice, gratitude, perpetual rest-
lessness, and loss in many forms.

While I was reviewing the authors' submissions, I was surprised to find that they rarely described their negative immigration experiences through outbursts of raw emotions. They didn't seem to be sad or angry enough. Their voices were more acquiescent than defiant. I couldn't help but wonder: Were they afraid to let go? Did the immigrant label silence them? Did they see stigma and ill-treatment as inevitable side effects of immigrating? Or does the gratitude of being able to call Canada home trump everything else?

One of my motivations behind this book was my own lingering frustration and desire to tell someone (or everyone) that we all have come from somewhere. That immigrants are some of the most hardworking and driven individuals I have ever met. That they don't leave their home countries to take anything away from anyone. That they put time and effort into helping their new communities. That they sacrifice a great deal for a chance for a better future.

Canada is a land of immigrants, and apart from the Indigenous people, everyone has an immigrant story somewhere in their history. My hope is that sharing these stories will help immigrants in Canada and around the world increase their sense of belonging and perhaps numb the persistent loneliness. I also invite those who do not identify with the immigrant label to engage in a critical reflection on what it means to be a Canadian immigrant woman. May the courage of these women inspire you to pursue your own opportunities—whether in Canada or elsewhere.

Dear English Language

CAMILA JUSTINO (BRAZIL)

Hello English language,

Sometimes you look at me with this look as though you know everything. Indeed, you know. Everything is ruled by you. The laws, the signs and the human thoughts of this land. I try to touch you, you have this nice sound, you are a superstar, the Hollywood celebrities use you, you travel the world in chart-leading hits that people cheer even without knowing you well. Sometimes I wish you were part of me but you keep being a strange body.

We don't belong to each other, we don't have this intimacy but still you are very close to me, you are waves inside my body yet you claim and attack my mother tongue for every failure. Sometimes you have moments of saying particular things in my head. *How could you write using me, you don't know how to channel me.* Then you ask me to stop using you so vaguely, so poorly. *You are an immigrant,* you repeat over and over. Sometimes you say, *You are beautiful,* and I get surprised, and suddenly I realize it's not really you, it's the song I listen to on the radio.

You name me an immigrant and when I am an immigrant I am nothing else.

An immigrant exists to be a character, or to be a cover on newspapers (with a suffering face in a suffering manner), or to be the cover of *The Immigrant Woman Magazine*, or to be part of the statistics (How many of them do we have here?), or to be a topic studied in university, or to be a theme for a conference, or to be helped by non-governmental organizations, or to be interviewed for institutional videos, or to be helped by the church, or to be a beneficiary of government funding, or to receive honours on TV, or to be included in politicians' speeches, or to be represented in human rights books. You keep saying it. And when I try to explain all this, you run away. You put a lot of ideas in my mind and then vanish.

Ha ha! You laugh at me in these moments. *I gave you this label gently,* you whisper. *What would you be without me giving you this label? It's for the best, take advantage of being an immigrant.*

You are sharp, but then you say I am doing a great job. You probably say this after feeling sorry for me. Then you suddenly change, you become polite and try not to compare me with who is from here, who can use you with fluency. It is easier to feel sorry for me. I accept all your words because I don't know how to argue with you. I just would like to say that I hate when you say I am doing a great job.

We are admired for virtues that we ourselves will never understand, living all the circumstances of leaving a motherland, of leaving a language that will never forget us. Now I am like broken glass and you put up all the pieces the way you want. Because I know how to scrub the floor very well, because I lack language and money.

We weren't born to write all our own stories using you. *Let someone else do it. Get a translator*, you keep knocking on me, sometimes you are like a serpent, you escape when I try to speak or write using you. You come and you leave.

Sometimes I try to ignore you. I breathe with relief and my mother tongue comes with her warm words, she hugs me but then she says it's for my best if she leaves me. *English is not so bad*, she tells me, *he is objective and also has a very good humour, he loves you in a different way, but he does love you.* I tell my mother tongue you accuse her of every failure but somehow she says you have your own reasons. *Do you know "tough love"?* she says with a funny accent. "Tough love" is an expression that can't be translated to my mother tongue but she guesses the meaning with her intuition. *Tough love, that's what English feels for you.* She comes to visit me less and less for my own good. I have saudade, a word followed by a feeling that can't be translated exactly to you, but I can tell you it is a verb that means empty of somebody that fulfills you somehow. Maybe one day you and mother tongue will get along.

I feel empty. Sometimes I call you or mother, but you are not there. Why? I have visited this limbo many times, there is no language at all. Where are you guys?

With no language I use the signs. I pay attention on eyes, mouths, bodies, lines, objects. If they are smiling, I just keep smiling and follow the tones to survive. And be grateful, don't forget you are in their land. Don't forget you got the permission to live (to survive) here.

Giving me permission to stay in a safe part of the planet is a favour. And an obligation. I am a good argument for human rights.

You guys keep providing me with cute speeches, but when I need at least one of you to help me think, you are gone. I don't like these games. And since mother tongue left for a while with no sign of return, I am telling you, English, I am not accepting this anymore.

It took me a while to write this letter. I had these secret words, but I didn't know how to tell you. You will ask: *How could I save hidden words from you?* I decided not to be your servant anymore.

If you want to stay with me, stay truly. I am owning this space—my brain, my mind, my body. And if you want to fool around or if you want to represent me as a fool, I will laugh at you out loud. I will say *Ha ha, it's not me, it's the English who is fooling around with me.*

And don't be surprised if I say words that you don't want to say. Also don't feel surprised if I don't repeat things you ask me to repeat.

No, I don't want to be translated in the community centre or in the doctor's office and I will not say, *Sorry, I don't speak English.* I will say, *Sorry, English is learning how to go through me.* And if you disappear again I will say, *Sorry, English is gone, you know … he likes to play games sometimes.*

I will not cover your games. Not this time, silly.

I don't want to be represented by a class or by a label chosen by you. I am not just an immigrant. I am not just a woman, a mother or a man. I am all of it. I am none. I am not a character. I am writing you!

Do you understand, English?

Cheers,

From you know who

Previously published in GUTS, in June 2016

Displaced Person

GINA ROITMAN (GERMANY)

In 1949, when I was nineteen months old, we sailed from Europe to Canada on the HMS *General Black*. We took Hitler along with us on the journey. Although I was too young to know it at the time, we were stuck with him for good. Wherever we went, my parents would drag his dead body with them, sitting him down at the kitchen table for a meal or on the couch as we watched old war movies.

In 1949 the *General Black* was just one of hundreds of freighters and ex-troop ships spilling some one hundred thousand DPs onto Canada's shores. These people were just like us: Displaced Persons who had been driven or expelled from their homelands by war, famine, tyranny or all of the above. World War II created an overabundance of DPs, a wave that has since swelled into a worldwide tsunami.

We had left the American-run DP camp in Germany where my parents met, and where they had conceived me. I was their main reason to hope that life could continue despite what they had lost. They left Europe, never to return. Nothing but ash and graves remained there, unattended, until some forty years later when I went in search of my history.

We arrived at Pier 21 in Halifax, Canada's Ellis Island, where we sat with so many others waiting to be processed. During the voyage, I had shared a crib with another baby, and as I was bereft of cousins, aunts and uncles, Issie, my crib mate, would become my ship-brother and his older sister, Gita, my ship-sister. I took our familial relationship seriously, but since they had arrived with an abundance of living relatives, I don't think they did.

Once processed at Pier 21, we were transferred to a train waiting outside, and then chugged along to Montreal, which has been my home ever since. And my history, lacking anything other than the charred stump of a family tree, began there, in the company of Hitler and the stories I didn't want to hear about a world that had been incinerated. I always thought of myself as a part of that generation Don McLean sang about in "American Pie": "There we were all in one place/A generation lost in space."

ooooo

My longing for some personal history began in 2000 with a casual revisit to Pier 21, now a national museum. Walking through the cavernous, almost empty hall, I read the panels and recognized in the stories the familiar mixture of hope and sadness. It's inherent in every immigrant tale about what was lost or left behind, mingled with what might be found or formed in this new land, not yet home.

In the centre of the exhibit stood two banks of pews, and facing them, an old wooden desk. I sat down and surveyed the immensity of the space, now so quiet, so empty, save for the stories of immigrants crowding the panels. But when I turned around, I was dumbfounded.

As if in a dream, I recognized the tableau. Above the desk was a sign, proclaiming in six languages: Welcome to Canada. But it was the little wooden desk that sparked a memory, a recollection of big block letters written in blue. Across the front of it, one word: IMMIGRATION.

I suppose our little family had sat there for a very long time. If I could recall the sign, I thought somewhat irrationally, what else was buried in my memory?

When you are without history, all you're left with is hope.

What if, I thought, I went back to my birthplace in Passau, Germany, or to Chrzanow, where my mother was born? By some miracle, could I dig up something of my past, some family history I could wrap myself in like a prayer shawl?

ooooo

When you grow up with a deficit of aunts, uncles and grandparents, jealousy rears its head on every birthday and holiday. And although on my father's side I did have two aunts, one lived in Israel and the other in Argentina—as far away from Montreal as the moon.

My mother methodically fed me family stories: about life in Poland before the war, what was lost and how she met my father. But my mother's stories were not what I wanted to hear. It was her road to sanity, but for me, a road littered with corpses. When she died in 1976, I believed that the stories, like all the dead relatives, had been laid to rest in the ground beside her.

Oddly, however, even today if you ask me where I come from, it is my parents' stories I tell—how my father left Belarus, a wife and three children when conscripted by the Soviet army. He went to Siberia, they went to Auschwitz. My mother and her husband escaped to Uzbekistan, where she had a son. Her husband died of malaria, her son of starvation. When my parents met, they married to begin life anew. I was the new, but in those days I didn't want the history.

Then in my forties, inexplicably, I wanted more than stories. I wanted facts, street addresses, genealogy that goes back past grandparents born in the 1800s. I wanted to ask questions and get answers. But whom to ask? Everybody was dead.

When I was young, I had hopes of being a journalist but quickly learned I wasn't very good at asking the tough questions. I became a publicist instead; putting a positive spin on things has always been my nature. Yet, suddenly, I would have gladly traded my rose-tinted glasses for a mere twig on the family tree.

So I planned an odyssey to my place of birth in Passau, Germany, and to Chrzanow, just fifteen kilometres north of Auschwitz. Somewhere I didn't want to go, but I had learned to leave all options open.

When you don't know what you're after, it's hard to make a concrete plan.

ooooo

My journey began in Munich, just two hours west of Passau, where I had friends. On my first day, my friend Elke and I walked through the town centre into the Marienplatz with its neo-Gothic town hall, the famous glockenspiel mechanical clock and the Frauenkirche with neat rows of window boxes, where blood-red geraniums splashed colour onto white walls. Afterwards, we meandered into the English Gardens, a testament to the German love of open spaces and biergartens. There are four in the nine-hundred-acre park in the centre of Munich. Elke chose the Chinesischer Turm. In the background, the Chinese pagoda, built in the eighteenth century, was enchanting, but eventually, and unbidden, the beer garden scene from the movie *Cabaret* began to play in my head. I heard the strains of a high, young voice beginning to sing "Tomorrow Belongs to Me." There I was, all these years later, and Hitler was still tagging along on my journey.

Guiltily, I glanced over at Elke, who had once asked me, "What must you think of us?" It was not a question that would ever be asked in Canada.

The next day, I took the train for a day trip to Passau. The town where I was born has buried its strong Nazi past, according to Anna Rosmus, a Passauer and the author of several books, including *Out of Passau: Leaving a City Hitler Called Home*. I was blasé about being a wandering Jew in Passau, having been to Germany several years before when the first sight to greet me in Frankfurt Airport was a pious Jew, facing west, saying his morning prayers wrapped in phylacteries and a tallis. I took that as an omen that it was safe to come back.

Passau is a little jewel of a town and I played the tourist because, although I was born there, I'm plainly not *from* there. (Just as I've lived in Canada most of my life but never felt I was from there either.) In a small shop adjacent to St. Stephen's, an exquisite baroque cathedral, I was startled to find a tiny Star of David with an amethyst in the centre. Leonardo da Vinci thought amethyst was able to dissipate evil thoughts. I bought the charm and placed it on my bracelet, ensuring I would have a story to tell when I got back to Montreal.

In Passau, three is a magic number. Three rivers in three colours—the black Ilz, the green Inn and the blue Danube—merge. Three countries—Germany, Austria and the Czech Republic—touch borders. And here my father, mother and their respective ghosts came together to form me.

Where no memories exist, I invent metaphors.

I roamed along the picturesque riverbanks and through the streets, taking photos of interesting architecture, but found nothing on which to hang a memory. But while heading back to the train station, I picked up one unforgettable souvenir. As I was passing a travel agency, I stopped to admire its window filled with maple leaf flags and signs touting the wonders of Canada. One stated simply: Human Nature. I caught my reflection superimposed on the Canadian flag and had to smile.

ooooo

Standing in the Jewish cemetery in Chrzanow, I held in my hand a piece of paper with the names of five Klugers who are buried there, the last one in 1924. Months earlier, in Montreal, I had optimistically printed the list off the JewishGen ancestry site, but I was no longer sure what I was doing in that cemetery. I had no idea how those names were related to me; I merely knew that my mother had been a Kluger, so these gravestones and I were somehow connected by the tenuous lines formed by six Hebrew letters. The memories she had passed on to me, and these names, were all I had to prove that I have roots—that I come from *somewhere* I could claim as mine. I wasn't from Poland, my mother's homeland, or Belarus, my father's. I was born in Germany. What history would I want to—or could I—claim from there?

Beside me a large snail trailed slime across a gravestone. My driver, Zniebiew, said that many tons of these fat, juicy snails were exported from Poland to France each year. I wondered if some were harvested in cemeteries like these.

I came to my mother's hometown of Chrzanow, thirty-five kilometres west of Krakow, looking for my roots, but I had very little to go on. In this neglected and overgrown Jewish cemetery, a thought wormed its way through the numbness I had worn as a mantle since arriving in Poland twenty-four hours earlier: the weeds seemed to have deeper roots here than I did.

In Chrzanow, there was nothing of my history left at all. After the cemetery, my driver took me to city hall, where a young man explained that all the records of local Jews had been destroyed during the war. Just in case someone made it back and wanted to reclaim their home or possessions. Only the cemetery remained, he said.

Unhappy with the answer, Zniebiew tried rephrasing the question, but there was not so much as a thread left to tie myself to that place. A kind man, he looked at me sadly. The young clerk also seemed sad to have disappointed me.

ooooo

Canadian-born, my ex-husband liked to bring me down a peg by calling me a mockie. In Jewish Montreal, it was a word that separated new immigrants arriving after World War II from the old ones who had come decades earlier and had established a life wedged between the English and French cultures. The derivation of the word is from the Hebrew mahkeh, meaning plague. We new immigrants were a plague, arriving as we did with our war stories and the shadow of Hitler behind us, told in thick accents and reminding those established of what they themselves had once been.

In Passau and Chrzanow, I was looking for the past, some connection to a line of people whose lives would help me connect to something other than stories. But what are we if not the sum total of all the lives lived in all the places where someone once came as an immigrant?

We are our stories.

I Come from a Word on a Map

MIRIAM MATEJOVA (SLOVAKIA)

Immigrants are permanent outsiders. Their past lives, experiences, skills and world views are often misunderstood, ignored or discarded in their new countries. Their old homes, no longer "theirs," become not much more than a fading memory. Their new homes, not yet "theirs," are the grounds of an everyday struggle for acceptance.

I am an immigrant. In formal correspondence I refer to myself as a naturalized Canadian. My friends teasingly call me a foreigner. My Canadian partner sometimes introduces me as a "halfie." Even after twelve years, my mother, who has never emigrated, refuses to accept any of the above.

Although I was born into the former Soviet Bloc, I have no thrilling emigration story to tell. No climbing through barbed wire, no sneaking in the shadows to cross a patch of unwatched border at night, no sewing of documents into car seats. I was a preschooler when the Wall crumbled, but I do have some memories of the communist times in former Czechoslovakia: beef and bananas that my grandmother used to get under the counter, gas street lamps with eerie green flickering light, and films where crowds of common workers randomly broke into catchy, proletariat-glorifying work songs.

I was eighteen years old when I was welcomed to Canada by a brisk Calgary winter. It was immediately obvious to me that my thin winter jacket, a loosely knit hat and mittens set and a pair of bright red (and barely waterproof) snow boots were not made for weather above the 48th parallel. In Bratislava, my hometown, winter is annoying—the wind whips your face, the rain gets in your eyes and the dampness sneaks into your bones. In Calgary, winter hurts. "Imagine this," I later told my family and friends back in Bratislava. "At minus ten, it's just really cold there. At minus twenty, your nose starts freezing from the inside when you breathe. At minus thirty, your eyelashes freeze together." They gaped. I beamed in their open acknowledgement of my newly acquired toughness.

But the stereotypical harshness of the Canadian winter is not the largest shock an immigrant may receive. Other baffling phenomena include cheerful bus drivers, the lack of female inhibitions about sporting slacks in public places, a general infatuation with peanut butter and that famous and frequently mocked Canadian politeness. The last one perhaps shocked me most, and not because of its mere existence, but because of my incredulous conviction that this superficial kindness was just that—superficial.

In Canada, I found kindness openly displayed in stores, at bus stops, at administration offices, with strangers proudly wearing it as a badge of their Canadian identity. Having grown up in a fundamentally opposite social system—in a nation stinting in kind words and generous with biting remarks—I eyed this kindness with sharp suspicion, scrutinizing it, evaluating the level of its genuineness as low and, in the process, unintentionally backing myself into a self-imposed social vacuum. That isolation stung me more than Calgary's January wind.

There is a dark side to leaving one's home and making a new one within someone else's borders. An immigrant is a foreigner in her own home, whether it's the one she's abandoned or the one she's created anew. An immigrant is often excluded from the bubble that others live in. An immigrant is very quickly recognized for who she is, and then often judged for who she isn't. An immigrant is sometimes listened to with awe, her past life reduced to an abstract concept, a story from a word on a map. An immigrant feels perpetually guilty for leaving loved ones behind and for constantly failing to reach what she has left them for. An immigrant never stops being afraid of returning home to realize no one is waiting for her. An immigrant is forever lonely.

I often feel this loneliness crawling toward my heart, nesting itself at the top of my chest and from there spreading to other parts of my body. Often, it squeezes my throat as it advances to my face, freezing my features in a scowl. People then assume I am angry.

I am not angry. I am terrified of my inability to shake off uncertainty and its trusty sidekick, the pervasive fear of failure. The duo is draining, menacing; it feeds on my past choices and keeps casting an unnerving shadow that clings over the future like static plastic wrap.

I am not angry. I am fragmented. I never cease to feel the incessant pull of two worlds. The first is the one where I keep returning with the anticipation of finding it the same as when I left it. The Danube River slightly less polluted, the spaces between concrete high-rises filled with fewer new constructions, the city's walking trails less neglected, a neighbourhood bakery still selling fresh plum cakes, a neighbourhood boy not commemorated by a plastic cross placed at the intersection that took his life.

In the other world, I am a stubborn woman with a European accent and a tendency toward outbursts of unfiltered thoughts. I can buy a cup of coffee every day. I can put up Christmas decorations in November without cringing at spoiling a family tradition. I can eat summer produce in winter. I cherish my ability to choose the hockey team I want to support, the traditions I want to adhere to and those I want to dismiss. That ability tastes like freedom.

The friction from the inter-world tugging has, however, left a hollowed-out space in which I now exist. Canada has dulled the sharp edges of my tongue and prompted me to smile at strangers. But Canada has also injected me with a sense of distrust. Now, when I return to Bratislava, the streets seem narrower, the alleys darker. The patches of urban grass, framed with cracked urban concrete, have faded from lush green to a dull yellow. Bus drivers are not cheerful, servers at restaurants rarely smile and commuters at bus stops don't initiate conversations.

In Canada, upon hearing me speak, strangers ask me where I am from, and I struggle to find the most accurate answer. My home is not a distinct spot on a map. My culture can hardly be expressed by a simple definition. My "self" does not belong to a single place, but is splintered, its fragments scattered across two diverse countries, cultures, worldviews, as well as the space between them. My mother refuses to call me a naturalized Canadian, a foreigner or a halfie. Regardless, that is who I am: a foreigner, a dreamer, a deserter, a visitor, a spectre of my former self clinging to the future while refusing to let go of the past. I am an immigrant.

Previously published in *The Rain, Party, & Disaster Society*, in September 2016

Other People's Houses

JOSEPHINE BOXWELL (THE UNITED KINGDOM)

We land in an unfamiliar location. Suburbia. A suitcase each and enough memories to make us homesick for all the places we've lived. I am the immigrant; she is from the other side of the country. Southern Ontario is foreign to both of us.

My partner has a cousin here who has welcomed us into her home. The cousin's house is surrounded by flatness. Fields hit the horizon, except where they have been eaten up by strip malls, big-box stores and uniform housing estates. I learn new words for coins and branded donut holes and coffee with lots of sugar and cream. The roads are wider, the vehicles are bigger and public transit is complicated. It isn't what I expected. Where are the mountains? Where is the Canada of the tourist ads: clean and green and pumped full of wildlife?

The cousin and her wife are doing their best to fit in here with their kid and cats and dogs and seven-seater SUV. They try to emulate this suburban "normal." Their neighbours believe the pair are mother and daughter, what with the age gap and the fact that the neighbours' assumptions have never been corrected. It is an uncomfortable feeling, not fitting in. Normal is so empty. I want to go home.

My parents contact me on Skype. They're calling from the old brick house I grew up in, in a town that sits between two rivers and the Irish Sea. That house has been in our family long enough to gather stories. My great-grandparents bought the place after the Wall Street Crash swallowed up what was left of the family business. It was the house my grandparents took my dad home to after he was born. I have early memories of visiting my great-aunt there before we moved in. She had a sitting room upstairs where she served afternoon tea with cake that had been left out long enough to grow mould. There was no central heating in the house at that time, and it smelled like musty curtains. The loo roll was like tracing paper. I imagined my great-aunt had stockpiled it during the war. No one else had toilet paper like that.

My parents tell me all about the weather and their current pre-occupations. They are busy removing the asbestos from the roof outside my bedroom, below the tall sash window that rattled throughout my childhood. Sometimes I'd open it and climb out onto the roof and sit there for a while, because it was somewhere I shouldn't have been. It won't be there the next time I visit. They're going to put a balcony in. They'll send photos.

My partner and I navigate our way out of suburbia. We move to St. James Town, Toronto, into a sixties concrete block full of new immigrants. There are no nice SUVs or labradoodles or patches of grass upon which to obliterate dandelions. We sublet from a friend of a friend's ex. He's away for a month visiting family in Korea, and his place got broken into recently, so he could do with the extra cash.

His apartment is white and pristine. White walls, white leather couch, white kitchen, white shelves. The sparseness is disturbed only by the mountain of hair products in the bathroom (he's a stylist by trade). There's a handful of framed photographs and they are all of him and his ex-boyfriend. His home is not ours, and in it he keeps hold of something that is no longer his.

We move on to a basement suite in a townhouse. Our new address: Queen West. Hipsters and young professionals convene here. The cafés all write chalky statements on sandwich boards about life or locally sourced lunch specials or their bold refusal to offer Wi-Fi.

It's a beautiful old house on a tree-lined street; another sublet. There are two tenants down here and another three upstairs. We all share the kitchen, and each floor has a bathroom. The tenant we're subletting from is a touring opera singer, and she has left her hair in the carpet. Her books are on the shelves. Her blankets are on the bed. She is someone who comes and goes. Her residences are only ever half-homes, half-occupied, used to store the things she cannot carry around. Her stories, I assume, go with her on the road. There are no photos or personal touches on these walls. In no time at all, she returns and we are displaced again.

My parents call. Mum has redecorated the living room. They've taken out the old fireplace and put in a wood-burning stove. They swing the laptop screen around to try and show me, but I can't make out much between the blown-out lights that throw the rest of the frame into shadow. Mum tries to describe the colours on the walls to compensate for the poor-quality video. The only thing I can tell for certain is that it is not how it was, and I'm not sure I like it.

We cross the city to Toronto's east side, the messy bit that's undergoing an identity crisis as house prices explode. Moms push their seven-hundred-dollar jogging strollers past long-haired men rolling their bin-bagged possessions in shopping carts. A boutique donut shop pops up beside a trashy diner. Choose your poison: hipster treats, or bacon with guaranteed sulphates and rehydrated eggs.

We rent a room in a house occupied by multiple others. Students mostly, and a male burlesque dancer. We go to one of his shows: A Funeral for Church Street. It is a tribute to the gay district as it once was (it was much gayer, apparently). The city's distinctive neighbourhoods are being eroded, threatened by the sameness that those in the suburbs seem so desperate to maintain.

Our room has a desk, a borrowed television and a single bed. I roll over the first night and smack my head into the wall. There is a faint electrical hum in the kitchen and the front steps are rotting out. We watch the raccoons climb up the fire escape and listen to them scurrying around in the roof above us, fighting, feeding their babies. This is their home. The rest of us are still in transition.

My parents call. They're tearing down the outbuildings. They are falling down anyway, they say. I ask them not to. They are part of my childhood, those crumbling bricks and slate roofs. It isn't my home anymore, though, is it? If it isn't, then where is?

Our landscape shifts again. I lose the right to work. I can remain in the country while my permanent residency application continues to be processed, but only as a visitor. My partner finishes her studies and finds a job, but it isn't local.

We put our two suitcases, a guitar and a bicycle on the train and ride across the country. I finally see the mountains *and* a moose. It is much more than I imagined. We settle in a quiet little village in the desert in a Canada I never knew existed. Ranches and sagebrush and tumbleweed.

Out here, we can afford to rent an entire house. It comes with a garden and two cats and a music studio in the basement, and it's ours for a whole six months while the homeowner, a musician, tours the country. She got divorced recently. Her ex-husband has returned to Vancouver and she has taken off for a while with her songs.

Once a month, the community piles into our rented living room to host a house concert series. There's a committee in charge. We don't have to do anything except open the door. The musicians are folky and bluesy, and they come from all over Canada and the United States. They know what it's like to be separated from home by choice, out of love. None of us can stay here, though. This house is still trapped in a financial and emotional mess. It is no one's home.

We move again.

My parents call.

You, in Translation

Margaret Nowaczyk (Poland)

> The poet moves from life to language, the translator moves from language to life; both, like the immigrant, try to identify the invisible, what's between the lines, the mysterious implications.
> —Anne Michaels, *Fugitive Pieces*

> Translate (physics)—to cause a body to move so that all its parts travel in the same direction, without rotation or change of shape.
> —*Oxford English Dictionary*

You list your family's needs for the first week in Toronto: subway tickets, bed linens, childcare for your six-year-old sister, translation of your father's university diploma and of your high school report cards. The Polish interpreter at the Ontario Welcome House utters four rapid words to your immigration caseworker that you don't catch. A crash course on the difference between an interpreter and a translator.

ooooo

Your caseworker snaps: "*We* say 'please' at the *end* of the sentence" just as you say: "Please would you ..." Her kilt swirls about her knees as she turns, sashays away and leaves you standing in the middle of the waiting room at the Welcome House.

You instruct your new classmates and teachers on how to pronounce your Polish name—maw-goh-JAH-tah. They mangle it and say: "It's beautiful." After a year of suffering their garbled utterances, you begin to introduce yourself as Margaret. No more exotica—you want to blend in, to belong, in name if not in anything else.

ooooo

While discussing *Heart of Darkness*, where she disapproves of Conrad's usage of "moustaches," Miss Anglin, your grade-twelve English teacher, announces that immigrants may become bilingual after many years, but that their English will never be idiomatic. You're the only non-English-speaker in the class—of course you take it personally.

ooooo

You miss hearing people laugh at those one-line zingers you were famous for.

ooooo

After you get a "marginal pass" on the written English proficiency exam required after the university admission, an alumnus of a Toronto private school even you have heard of can't stop laughing: he got the same mark.

ooooo

"Omit needless words," Strunk and White admonish. But you need to know these words first, you think dejectedly.

ooooo

You stun your brilliant Canadian boyfriend by asking whether "lousy" comes from "louse"—it never occurred to him. You have to show him in the library copy of the *Oxford Dictionary of English* that "a lot" is two words, not one: he wouldn't take your word for it.

ooooo

When you read the journal you write in English, in your head it sounds as if filtered through a mouthful of pebbles.

A Canadian guy at the Harbourfront Castle bar tells you that you speak English really *good*. The irony is not lost on you, even if your accent gives you away again.

ooooo

You smirk after reading "The Owl and the Pussycat"; it's cute, precious. You read the Polish translation and you burst out laughing—it's funny! A lightning-fast punch in your gut. In your native tongue, "a hog 'cross a road" evokes emotions and memories where "and there in a wood a Piggy-wig stood" fails.

ooooo

When you meet the man you will marry and bear two sons for, he introduces himself as James. Like you, he has changed his name; he was given a Greek one at birth. You never call him Demetrios, and he never calls you Małgorzata.

ooooo

For a long while, you can't indulge in puns or neologisms anymore—Canadians correct you because your accent belies your grasp of the language. When you go back after twenty-one years, you aren't allowed to do it there, either—you are corrected because Poles think you've forgotten your native tongue.

ooooo

You write and publish a book in Polish. It becomes very popular, but why does it feel like a step back?

ooooo

When you travel to Poland, you sometimes speak Polish to your sons and then insist that you've spoken English. They shake their heads—no, you haven't. They don't understand Polish—their father's ancestry is Greek, and therefore your language of love and child-rearing is, by default, English.

ooooo

A professional English translation of your book—you don't recognize the voice. But in a short story you write in English, your voice finally sings.

"Do you still speak Polish?" a venerable colleague at a medical meeting asks in his strong German accent. "I'm bilingual," you answer after a moment's hesitation. After twenty-three years, finally a correct word to describe yourself.

Soldiers

AYELET TSABARI (ISRAEL)

Ali and I are playing backgammon on a coffee-splattered table outside
Caffé Roma on Commercial Drive. It's an unseasonably warm winter day, a blue-skied wonder in this city of grey and glass, the kind of
day that makes foolish Middle Eastern people like us rejoice in global
warming. I light a cigarette, sip my double espresso and watch Ali. He's
squinting at the board, brow furrowed. Then he sighs and makes his
move, leans back in his seat and drinks from his cranberry juice.

Bouncing the dice in my hand, I scan the board and size up the
layout, taking note of Ali's vulnerable spots. I throw the dice and after quick consideration—nothing says amateur more than counting
spaces—I go on the offensive, break a house and take down Ali's soldier. I place his casualty on the bar in the middle of the board with a
self-satisfied grin, blowing smoke to the side.

Ali stares at the board and frowns, his lazy eye slow to blink.
"What are you doing?"

"Kicking your ass."

"You're not thinking. You can build a house."

"I know. I don't want a house."

"But you're leaving yourself open—"

"I know what I'm doing." I knock back the rest of my coffee.
"Are you seriously telling me how to play backgammon?"

We've had this argument before. Ali loves to speak of Iraqi su-
periority when it comes to backgammon. After all, they played it on

the banks of the Babylon River for thousands of years. I have little patience for his speech: I take backgammon seriously, and I'm good at it. It's one of many skills I acquired in my years of travelling and lounging in coffee shops—skills I cannot put on any resume, like rolling joints while driving, bargaining in bazaars or getting by in foreign countries with hardly any money. I tell him about the tournament I won in India, my hours-long winning streak—a story I'm fond of because it makes me sound like a legend. They were all men, too, lining up to play against me. One of them, a Turkish guy, kept coming back and losing until he stood up and yelled, "You're making me mad!"

Ali has heard the story before.

We both refer to the pieces as soldiers, don't know that in English they're named checkers, or pieces, because in our respective languages, soldiers is what they're called. Ali and I were both soldiers once, in our own countries, both drafted without a choice shortly after the First Gulf War, after his country launched Scuds at mine, and my country—miraculously and uncharacteristically—resisted the urge to retaliate. But my service, as traumatic as it seemed at the time, was in an administrative base in Tel Aviv, steps from a busy street with trendy restaurants and beautiful people in fashionable clothes. Ali's was not as cushy.

Ali's stories are always better than mine. I tell him about the summer it was so hot in my suburban town that when I stuck out my tongue, my chewing gum started bubbling. He tells me of scorching Baghdadi summers, days so hot that you'd fill the tub with ice and it melted as soon as you got in.

Ali throws the dice and looks at the board. He leans forward, casually resting his wrist on my knee.

"Hey," I say. "You think I don't know what you're doing? That's real low."

He shakes his head and laughs. Again, he opts for the safest move, the conservative option. When it's my turn, I shake the dice in my closed fist, kiss it for good luck and roll a double. I advance farther, leaving my exposed soldier defenceless. Ali bites his tongue.

He wins the game. He's trying not to be smug about it. I hate losing. I tell him he plays boring and safe—that he plays to win, while I play for the love of the game. He laughs; he's heard that before too.

He walks me home through darkening streets. The sky turns the kind of brilliant cobalt blue that follows sunny days, a lighter shade of blue traces the edges of the mountains. The downtown's mirrored buildings glow with fading orange in the distance. When the temperature drops quickly, I hug my leather jacket and babble about my travel plans. For a few days I was set on Turkey. Then I remembered it's not actually warm this time of year. Not beach warm. "I'm thinking Mexico," I say. At the Mexican restaurant where I work—hired because the Chinese owner thought I was Latin—people repeatedly ask me for their bill in broken Spanish. I've learned a few phrases.

We stop by the blue wooden gate outside my home. I grab Ali's hand. He doesn't pull away. His hands are always warm and mine always cold. I tell strangers it's a sign of a warm heart, although it is more likely a sign I should quit smoking. I smile at Ali. "Want to come in?"

"I can't."

I let go of his hand, resist a sigh. I don't say, "Call me." I know he won't.

Home is a basement suite off Commercial Drive that I've been sharing with two Egyptian sisters from Nova Scotia. Before I met Leyla, I was walking the streets of Vancouver, searching for a reason to stay. I had just turned twenty-nine. The few friends I had in the city had all left for one reason or another. I missed home, but couldn't imagine going back to Israel to live. My last lengthy stay was during the second intifada, and months later I was still startled by the sound of firecrackers on Halloween; I still boarded buses scanning for threats. Every time I caught a glimpse of news from Israel on a random TV screen or heard snippets on the radio, my muscles tensed. I took on extra shifts at the restaurant. As soon as I made enough money, I was going to pack up my backpack and head somewhere warm.

Then I met Leyla at a belly dancing class in the community centre. She was the only one in class who hummed to the music, sang along with the lyrics, whose body, like my own, knew the dance moves by heart. That first night we had coffee after class and talked about politics, about the wars between my country and that of her family, the history of bloodshed and hatred that bonded us. We hung out again the following week, and the next. We fell into friendship like some people fall in love, quickly, deeply, as though we recognized in each other something of ourselves. When my lease ran out, Leyla and her sister, Rana, offered their couch.

On Commercial Drive, Leyla and I became a fixture. Whenever I went to Caffe Napoli without her, the barista asked, "Where's your wife?" When we walked down the street arm in arm, Leyla with a colourful hijab framing her face, the Algerian men outside Abruzzo café jerked their chins toward me, whispering in Arabic, "Hiya Yahoodia." She's Jewish. What they were saying was, "See those two Arabic-looking girls? They are not what they seem." What they were saying was, "What are these two doing walking arm in arm?" I translated for Leyla, whose Arabic was not as good as mine, and we both glared. Secretly we were pleased with the attention, with the confusion we caused, with complicating their notions of Jews and Muslims, Israelis and Egyptians.

Leyla introduced me to her friends. Ibrahim was a joker with a curly 'fro and a taste for fashion, a gifted painter who'd studied art at the University of Baghdad; Firaz, quieter, more thoughtful, also an Iraqi immigrant, worked in computers. My new friendships felt easy, a slice of home replanted in this foreign land. Our kitchens smelled the same; our music used the same scales, the same beat. Their language was the language of my grandparents, who had emigrated from Yemen to Israel in the 1930s—a language I resisted studying in school, learning to associate it with the enemy rather than with my own heritage. During my first year in Vancouver, I heard Arabic spoken on the bus once and tensed instantly. Then I looked back and saw two young students—a boy and a girl—chatting in the back seat. It was the first time I came face to face with my own prejudice, my own deep-seated fear. I had no idea how deeply ingrained it was.

In finding Leyla and her friends, I discovered something in me that had lain dormant: the Yemeni identity I had rejected as a child, growing up in a country that suppressed Mizrahi traditions, educated in a school system that focused on Ashkenazi history and literature.

In Vancouver, I didn't feel a part of the Jewish community— mainly Canadian and Ashkenazi. Most people I met in the city had never encountered a Yemeni Jew and didn't know what to make of me. To Canadians, Jewish meant delis and lox and matzo ball soup, as exotic to me as a Woody Allen movie. At parties, upon finding out I was Jewish, people asked if I spoke Yiddish.

I began thinking of myself as an Arab Jew, finding it wonderfully romantic and contentious, tasting it on my tongue, surprised by how easily it rolled off. I became obsessed with my Middle Easternness, infatuated with my Arabness. On the bus to work I read *A History of the Modern Middle East*, highlighter in hand, listening to Fairuz and Umm Kulthum on my headphones, dreaming of travelling to the Middle East with my yet-to-be-acquired Canadian passport, taking courses at the University of Cairo, learning to belly dance from Nagwa Fouad and Mona Said.

Ali was Firaz's new roommate. A recent immigrant from Iraq, he was the most conservative of the bunch; he didn't smoke, didn't drink—not for religious reasons, he insisted when I pressed one night in a drunken attempt to flirt. He just didn't like to lose control. He dressed like my accountant uncle—a Lacoste shirt tucked into eighties-wash jeans. His hair was receding and he sported a moustache before it was fashionable to do so. But he had a beautiful, strong profile, dramatic features, broad shoulders and a manly, confident walk. He had a dimple in one cheek and a lazy eye I found irresistible. His accent was subtle, sexy, and every now and then a guttural *k* slipped into his English, like the *q* at the end of Iraq, a sound alien to most Canadians, impossible to pronounce, but I knew it from Iraqi friends' parents or grandparents in Israel. And his hands—they were big and dry and warm. Whenever he touched me, which he rarely did, and so briefly that I thought I'd imagined it, they applied pressure, meaning.

ooooo

At home, Leyla is making us dinner, roasting an eggplant for baba ghanouj, tossing salad greens with lemon and olive oil and za'atar. She shakes her head as I talk about Ali. "I know you miss home," she says. "And he may look like it, but he's not it."

Leyla is scary smart. Sometimes it's intimidating, other times infuriating. At twenty-three she has already lived in half a dozen countries. She became a Muslim of her own volition on a trip to Africa; her secular Egyptian parents hadn't raised her that way. I don't understand her choice, but I admire her resolve. We talk about everything, question everything, including the hijab, including God, including my commitment issues, my inexplicable attraction to Ali.

"You have nothing in common," she says. Ali doesn't read. His favourite movie is *Analyze This*. He makes no sense in my world.

Still, we have the army. We have backgammon. We have summers and heat and food and music and language. To Leyla I say, "I know. It's physical, okay? It's not like I want him to be my boyfriend." Then, cheekily: "Think of it as my contribution to world peace." Leyla rolls her eyes. She does not dignify my quip with a response.

ooooo

The first time Ali and I hung out alone was at a peace march. George W. Bush had just announced his plan for invading Iraq, and worry about the impending war was palpable. Our friends were especially concerned; their families still lived there. We all met downtown and marched in the rain, yelling, "What do we want? Peace! When do we want it? Now!" We were buoyed by the energy of the crowd, intoxicated by the sounds of our voices becoming one with the mass, feeling strong, like we mattered.

By then we had gotten together as a group a few times, mostly at bars and a couple of art openings, and Ali and I spent some time chatting, or I did, uttering drunken nonsense I later regretted. At the peace rally we lost the group and found shelter from the rain in the lobby of an office building, where we finally had a serious, sober conversation. I took pictures of him that day. In one photograph he stands in front of the Vancouver Art Gallery like a tourist, stiff in his high-rise jeans and old-fashioned leather jacket. He had asked me to take that one. Another is a close-up shot of his Roman profile, looking away with a half-smile, appearing shy, self-conscious.

ooooo

One evening Leyla and I go to the apartment he shares with Firaz in Coquitlam to watch *The Prince of Egypt*. We end up staying past the SkyTrain closing hours, so Firaz and Ali lay out mattresses on the floor. Leyla and Firaz fall asleep beside us, but Ali and I stay up talking in whispers. We speak of our faraway, messed-up homelands, describing childhood smells and showing each other pictures.

We share stories from our days as reluctant soldiers, from sitting in shelters, listening to bombs or missiles falling, wearing gas masks. I tell him that my first suitor had arrived at our house with a gas mask during the Gulf War. "Thanks a lot for that, by the way," I say. Ali laughs so hard he can't talk.

Night sneaks in through a crack in the window, the smell of dry, cool air, of no rain. We rest our heads on the pillows. Ali glances at me sideways and starts singing, softly, in Arabic. I close my eyes and give in to the honeyed sound of the throaty, familiar syllables. I fall asleep to it as though it were the sweetest lullaby.

In the middle of the night we cling to each other, and Ali strokes my body with warm, large hands. A storm begins brewing in my belly. Then it all ends before it starts. "Go to sleep," he says, when I turn to him.

"Why?"

"It's better that way."

I wake up in the morning wondering if I had dreamt it all.

ooooo

"Why don't you ever call me?" I ask him the next time we meet. After the night I stayed over, he disappeared. Weeks went by. The one time we were all supposed to get together, he cancelled last minute, leaving a message on Ibrahim's phone.

We are sitting on the swings at Grandview Park. Our friends are at Bukowski's, now our regular bar. When I had stepped outside for a smoke, I asked Ali to join me, then grabbed him by the hand and brought him here, to the park. It's my spot. I have been coming here at night since summer. I'd smoke a joint, swing as high as I could, and watch the city lights flicker in the distance. Sometimes an arctic wind would sneak under layer after layer of clothing, stabbing me with ice needles, and I'd be seized by a sweet pang of loneliness, the thrill of anonymity. I'd look around with surprise that I was here, of all places. Half a world away from home. Alone. Free.

"Do you want me to call you?" Ali says.

"Isn't that obvious?"

"You left that morning without saying goodbye," he says. He does not look at me.

"I left a note. I had to go to work."

"You should have woken me up."

We swing side by side until we tire and slow down. I grab the rope of his swing and pull myself closer to him. I can smell his cologne: fresh, sharp.

"So … Mexico," Ali says, out of nowhere.

"Oh, no. I changed my mind," I say. "I think I should go east. Thailand maybe. It makes more sense."

"Of course." He stands up, brushes off his jeans. "Shall we go back?"

Disappointment sours my mouth.

That night, on the phone from Israel, my sister calls me a heartless bitch—in the nicest of ways. It's four in the morning Vancouver time; on the other end I hear traffic, the hum of midday Tel Aviv. Earlier that day a bomb had killed eleven civilians on a bus in Jerusalem. But my sister never mentions such things and I never ask. I sit on the bench outside the apartment door, lean my head against the wooden panels and chain-smoke.

"Do you think that maybe he likes you?" she asks. "Maybe he doesn't show it in the way you're used to. He's from a different culture."

She's right, of course. Ali is different from any guy I've ever met. It's like he is from a different generation altogether. The East Van hippie boys are so much easier.

"Just be careful," she says.

When I wake up the next morning, I am overcome by hangover and remorse. I regret the stupid things I say when I'm drunk, sorry for coming on too strong, for leading him on. I tell myself to let Ali go, move on.

That weekend, Leyla and I go dancing at a Middle Eastern night at the Anza Club. A guy in white pants, hair smoothed by too much gel, zeroes in on me. He tells me he's from Lebanon. He is movie-star-handsome and he knows it, dancing around me, singing to me with animated facial expressions, hand mocking his beating heart. The whole thing is over the top. Still, when he asks, I give him my phone number just to see his reaction. He stares at my name on the note with a frown, abandoning the theatrics. "Where are you from?"

"Israel," I say and watch the smile fade from his face.

Sometime at the end of that fall, Leyla takes off her hijab. One day I come home and her curls, tightly wound, are free. She's always been stunning. Now she is luminous.

We spend Christmas together, a few Muslims, one Jewish girl and Rana's boyfriend, who is Anglo-Canadian. We cook turkey with all the fixings. The Christmas before that is a distant memory: I had spent it alone, eating ice cream, reading *Vanity Fair* and wondering why I was even in Canada. This is better.

Leyla steals sips from my wineglass. She has borrowed my low-neck blouse, my dangly earrings and tight jeans. At some point in the night, she stands at the doorway smoking my cigarettes, blows smoke to the side and announces, "Look at me, I'm Ayelet." Everyone laughs.

Ali and I are cordial. I don't touch him. I don't flirt.

After dinner, the boys teach us a traditional Iraqi game called Mheibis. Rana volunteers her ring and Leyla one of her silk scarves. Generally played in two teams, the boys modify the rules to accommodate a smaller group. One player walks by and covertly slips the ring into someone's hands. Another player has to find the ring while the rest of us exercise our best poker faces. It is a game of deception and trickery, of careful observation. Psychological warfare. The player in charge of finding the ring can interrogate, manipulate or intimidate in order to expose the ring bearer. When it is Ali's turn to hide the ring, he stops by me and looks me in the eye long enough for me to miss a beat. His hand grabs mine under the cloth. He does not slip the ring into it. I do my best to mask my relief.

On New Year's Eve we go to Bukowski's and some drunken girl asks us if we are all one family. "No, we're just all Arabs," Leyla says. But then we look at each other and smile. We do look a little bit like family. When it's midnight, we hug and kiss each other on the cheek. Ali's lips just barely miss mine. I look at my feet.

In January a bomb explodes in Tel Aviv's central bus station, killing twenty-three. My family doesn't call. Leyla and I march from Library Square to the Vancouver Art Gallery with thousands of people chanting "Stop the War," and "Drop Sanctions, not bombs." Protestors form a drum circle on the steps of the art gallery. We listen to a lecture about the UN sanctions against Iraq at Simon Fraser University. We attend a candlelight vigil. It feels good to be a part of a movement, to be engaged in something positive, proactive, when back home every-thing is such a disaster. Doing this makes me feel a little less helpless.

When we go out at night, Leyla starts ordering her own drinks. At home, she smokes my pot. The two of us get rowdy at Super Valu while shopping for Nutella. We stumble back home from the bar sing-ing our hearts out. One day, stoned, we look at *The Province*'s cover page in a newsstand and see a picture from a peace rally we attended the day before. Leyla leans in and squints at the wide-angle photo of the crowd. "Look!" she gasps. We are right in the middle of the photo, two tiny figures, mouths open in mid-chant, chins raised, expressions focused, earnest. We bend over laughing, tears in our eyes. I glance at the photo again; I love seeing the two of us captured on the page, our friendship, our intentions, eternalized. We belong there; we fit.

I don't see Ali for a while.

Leyla starts dating a friend I introduced to her. A woman.

"You know you're going to hell, right?" Ibrahim tells me. Every-one laughs.

"They're calling me the Jewish devil," I complain to Leyla. "They say it's all my fault. The hijab. The drinking."

Leyla gives me a look. "Well, you did break my prayer stone."

"That was an accident!"

She holds back a smile.

One night, we lie together in her bed, talking. We've been shar-ing body products and laundry detergent and bed sheets for so long that we even smell the same, the way siblings and lovers do. Leyla lies on her side, examining me. "What would you do if you stayed?"

I stiffen. I think about things like school and writing and real jobs and immediately feel like the air is sucked out of the room. "I don't know."

"Sometimes I think you don't really want to go."

"What? Why?"

"You haven't given notice at work. And you don't have a ticket, or a plan."

But I have to go. Leaving is the only thing that I know to do. That seemed to be the one stable thing in my life, the ritual of pick-ing up, throwing out or giving away the little I have, packing and taking off. That was what home had become for me. But I think of leaving Leyla and my heart crumbles. It's a familiar ache. It's how I feel every time I leave Israel. My family.

Leyla lies on her back, looks at the ceiling. "There must be something so limiting and so lonely about needing to be free all the time."

When I tell my friends that I've decided to go to Montreal, they burst into laughter. "Montreal, in February? Are you nuts?"

But I've never experienced real winter and I'm curious. Besides, tickets from Montreal to Asia are dirt cheap.

It starts to rain, finally, after weeks of atypically dry weather, and I welcome it with gratitude, like something bottled has been released. I inhale the fresh smell of wet earth; I admire streaks of lights reflecting on the pavement.

Leyla is falling in love, and I hardly see her. Like with everything she does, she is passionate, committed. I envy her fearlessness, wonder how it feels to know something with such certainty, to believe in it with all you have, even when you fear it may not last. I can't even commit to a brand of cigarettes. I haven't seen our friends for a while. Perhaps they're busy, or perhaps Leyla was the glue that kept us together. After a few days the novelty of the rain wears off and it's another Vancouver winter: gloomy, wet to the bone.

In February I take my citizenship test, buy a one-way ticket to Montreal and move my stuff into storage: twelve boxes, a backpack full of clothes, one rolled mattress, a duvet in a garbage bag.

One day on the bus, a man sits next to me, smelling of Ali's cologne, and I suddenly ache for his warm hands, his winking eye, his guttural *k*. That evening I call him and invite him to a friend's birthday party, an Algerian girl I had also met at belly dancing class. I don't know why. Maybe it's because Leyla has been sleeping at her girlfriend's and I miss the sound of her key in the door, miss when she was my wife. Maybe it's because I'm leaving in a couple of weeks; what harm can it do now?

At the party, my friends—most of them immigrants themselves—don't know what to make of him, make of us. He stands out in his outdated attire, in his frozen smile—the smile I recognize from my first days in Canada, the smile I used to plaster on when I couldn't follow the speed of conversation, didn't get the joke, the cultural reference. He looks like he did in the picture I captured on the steps of the art gallery. When he passes the joint to me, he holds it out from his body, pinched between two fingers, like it is something both delicate and repulsive. I laugh out of tune with my friends, aware of his gaze, my discomfort exacerbated by the down-pull of the pot. On the way home he glances at me. "You shouldn't smoke so much pot," he says. He sneaks a warm hand into my cold one and my heart freezes.

I win our last backgammon game. It's a spectacular, satisfying win. Ali is graceful about it. He leans back, lazy eye winking. His gaze lingers on me, so full of warmth and affection that his sharply drawn face softens at the edges. I urgently reset the board and avoid his eyes.

Rain starts up on the way back home, fat, warm drops. We stand outside the house, saying goodbye. I'm about to give Ali a hug when he leans over and kisses me. At first I'm startled, but then I kiss him back and wrap my arms around him, let him lean me against the side of the house, let his hands travel under my clothes, onto my belly, my ribcage, the small of my back. He pulls away for a moment. "Let's go in," I say.

He steps away. "No."

"Why not?"

He hesitates, looks up at the rain. "You're leaving." He chews on the inside on his lip. "If I go in, I'll get more attached, and it will just hurt more."

We stand in the rain, wet, starting to shiver. The moment is gone. He plants a soft kiss on my lips, a period at the end of a sentence. Then he tucks his hands into his pockets and looks at me sideways, shaking his head and chuckling.

"What?"

"You know, you play backgammon like you live your life."

I raise my eyebrows.

"You play aggressively, you constantly take risks, you don't want to build houses. You leave yourself open all over the place, and when things get dicey, you run away."

I smile as if he has said something funny. I smile because I can't think of anything to say.

ooooo

This is where this version of the story ends, a version I wrote years ago, soon after Ali and I parted. This is where my memory chose to check out: Ali makes this insightful observation, which makes me feel seen, which makes me realize that perhaps I hadn't given him enough credit, and we part, never to see each other again. But reading through my diaries reveals a different ending. A part of the story I purposely forgot. It turns out I had reshaped the story into one I could live with. I had omitted the parts that exposed me, made me look like a jerk.

Toward the end of my army service, after numerous transfers and reassignments, I was stationed at a unit that worked to ensure safety in training. We dealt with accidents, with moments of inattention and thoughtlessness, with friendly fire, that careless and cynical phrase with its playful alliteration, not just an oxymoron but a crime of language, really. The lack of intent never mattered. Soldiers were hurt. If anything, it was all the more infuriating because it could have been prevented.

So, this is how our story really ends.

I have my goodbye-Vancouver party at the smoking room at Mona's Lebanese Cuisine, an establishment I love for its food and music and energy. I will end up working there for six years after I return from travelling, immersing myself in the Arabic community, becoming a part of the family who runs the place, feeling, finally, at home in the city.

That night, my friends and I smoke nargilas and drink arak, the room thick with apple-flavoured smoke and anise. Ali and I sit in the corner like a couple, his hand around my shoulder.

After the party, on the steps of my home, Ali tells me—a stone in his throat—that he has fallen for me, and my crush on him deflates as though pricked by a pin. For the next few days, as I get ready to leave, he is clingy, desperate. He calls, asks to accompany me on my final errands. He inquires about my plans for the future. I resent having to deal with this on my last few days in Vancouver. I say things like, "I am not looking for a boyfriend" and "I like you but not in that way." It is all too little, too late. He's not hearing me. In his world my flirting, my attention, can only mean one thing.

Women don't act this way unless they have serious intentions. I wish I had listened to my sister, to Leyla. I wish I could redo everything, and this time be good, be compassionate, be thoughtful. I can't shake the feeling that I liked the idea of Ali more than I liked Ali, that my contribution to world peace had little to do with the world and more to do with my need for instant gratification. My need for a good story.

He insists on taking me to the airport. By the gate, we hug. "I will miss you," he says.

I gaze at my feet. "Don't."

"I will anyway."

I will email Ali from Montreal, then Bangkok. I will be in a small fishing village on an island in the South China Sea when the United States invades Iraq. I will message Ali from an Internet café with no walls in the middle of a jungle, the smell of fish and salt permeating the humid air. He'll tell me he's heading back to Iraq, to be with his family. I will cry and wonder if maybe I have feelings for him after all.

A few months later, I will leave Thailand and fly to Israel, already infatuated with someone else. The memory of Ali will make me feel foolish and intensely guilty; I won't be able to recall the attraction. When I return from my travels a year later, Ali will be gone. Our friends will tell me that he never liked the rain. He moved to Italy, then the US. For a while our friends will keep me updated, until they too lose touch.

Sometimes he will pop up as a potential friend on Facebook. My heart will clench at the sight of his picture, his name. I will remember him. I will lower my eyes. I will mouth, *I am sorry*. Then I'll refresh the page and he'll be gone.

Previously published in *The New Quarterly*, in the summer of 2014

Nesting Dolls

Kaija Pepper (Russia)

When I was growing up, I could forget about my father all day while he was away at work. Dad was his own person then, driving a cement truck around town, and I don't suppose he thought about me. It was different with my mother. We were together at home every day and every night, and once I was old enough to go to school, though she was still there at home, she was still with me somewhere inside.

I was always inside her, too, along with my sister and brothers. Mom lived all our lives, starting when we were babies fresh from her womb, our newborn skin and bones like parts of herself, our smell her own as we sucked milk from within the warm cradle of her arms. One by one, we solidified into our singular selves—all four of us crawling and then walking away, away from her and toward the world. Yet something of each of us remained—our mother with us, and us with our mother.

There was another child inside Mom, one whose traces were deep in every cell in her body—Zinaida—her own young self. I had no notion of this other girl when I was little and Mom seemed big and powerful, a mother without beginning or end, just like the universe. It was only after her death that first my childhood, and then my mother's too, began to loom closer, as if the past were trying to be present all over again.

Zina took her first breath in Russia, in the midst of chaos as the family prepared to flee the Bolsheviks; in my mind it is the breath that has come to define her, though she grew up in China and, mostly, Canada. "My mother's Russian," I always said, and continue to say, using the past tense now that she is gone, because it's still how I think of her. "Russian" was the flavour Mom brought to our East Vancouver home, like the night she showed me how to cross myself in the Russian Orthodox fashion (up, down, right, left), which seemed superior to the way we did it at Beaconsfield United Church (up, down, left, right).

"Russian" was also the best explanation I had for the way she lived apart from the world around her. Despite her perfect English, Mom was like a foreigner who couldn't quite connect, unable to enter into the ebb and flow of an ordinary conversation.

At family suppers, Mom, Dad, my three siblings and I sat on blue vinyl swivel chairs crowded around a circular white Formica table. "Oi, there's too much racket," Mom groaned whenever the chatter became too enthusiastic. "We're here to eat, not talk."

When she did have something to say it was usually what we called nagging, which often became long rants that left no room for exchange, mostly about the many things keeping her from the peace and quiet she craved. Like me asking for something to eat when it was only a little while before dinner. Or my sister talking too long on the phone, stretching the cord from the kitchen where it was tethered, down the hall and into the bathroom, whispering behind the door. Or maybe Dad was arguing politics with a guest in the living room after Mom had gone to bed: "Oh, Andy, stop shouting!" she'd wail. Or my brothers and their friends were in the basement playing table hockey or darts, making such a racket she couldn't stand it anymore and screamed at everyone to go home. "Your mom's at it again," my friend said once as we stood outside my house, and I was shocked at how much you could hear from the street.

Every second summer, Dad drove us in the blue Parisienne across British Columbia to the Peace River district in Alberta to visit our Russian grandparents on the farm where Mom grew up. Before setting off, Mom would hand me a paper bag in case I got carsick, and my siblings and I would squabble over who got to sit beside a back-seat window. We'd play I Spy and spot out-of-province licence plates; by suppertime, Mom's nerves would be on edge. "We should stop and eat," she'd say anxiously as we approached a roadside diner.

Dad didn't seem to notice the tension in her voice, because, just like clockwork—or so it seems in memory, as if this scenario happened on every trip—he'd say, "I want to make it a little further. We have a lot of miles to go." Mom never learned to drive; he'd get no break behind the wheel.

Five or ten minutes later, moans from deep inside my mother would erupt, and soon she'd be crying, "Oi, my stomach, I can't take these hunger pangs."

There wouldn't be a diner in sight as Dad drove silently on. The inevitability of what was coming sunk me lower in my seat.

"I told you we should have stopped," Mom would wail. "You never listen, I need some nourishment!"

Dad focussed hard ahead while Mom groaned beside him on the highway that seemed to never end. A litany of woe rushed from her mouth: her hunger, Dad going his own way, us kids making too much noise, and no diner, when would there be another diner? "Jesus jumpin' catfish!" Dad would explode. "Zina, can't you just be quiet?"

Arriving at the farmhouse the next day, words I couldn't understand poured out of my mother's mouth: weightier vowels and consonants that had a different, unfamiliar rhythm. Russian, she was speaking Russian, and so were my grandparents, my uncles and aunts, all the Russian voices streaming together. The hot flow swirled around as I took stock of the old furniture and plain wood floors of the farmhouse, of the kitchen cupboards enclosed with thin cotton curtains hanging on string, of the chipped china plates and cups on which tea and cookies were served. I'd slip out to find the outhouse, following the dirt path to the wooden shack, fastening the door with the spindly wire hook, alone with the bugs and the smelly hole where I perched my bare bottom. At bedtime, I had to climb a ladder through a trapdoor in the ceiling to get to the attic where we kids bunked on the floor in sleeping bags.

At breakfast, Baba, a tiny, smiling woman in wire-framed glasses, spread my toast with pale, oily farm butter, nothing like the hard yellow margarine we used at home. Mom had to repeat in Russian whatever we said to each other.

Grandpa, who knew only a little more English, drove us into Hines Creek once for pop. After he parked the truck in town and we crossed the muddy, unpaved road, a gang of boys appeared calling Grandpa—a thin old man with a white beard—Father Christmas. Jeering, the boys followed us down the sidewalk, which was wooden, not cement like at home in Vancouver. Grandpa didn't say a word, not then, and not when we sat at the counter in the café sucking our sweet fizzy drinks through straws, the ice cream in my Coke float slowly melting. I don't suppose he said anything back at the farm, though I don't know what the adults talked about in Russian.

Dad, who was Finnish, wouldn't have known either. But he was a patient man, and next summer it would be his turn: we'd drive even farther east to Ontario to visit our grandparents in Port Arthur, when mysterious Finnish sounds would fill the air.

All during our visit, my mother's past was right next to me, but I never noticed: the farmhouse where she grew up was simply about our family vacation, my summer holiday. I didn't wonder back then if boys made fun of the bearded Russian men when she was a child. I didn't wonder where Mom's bedroom had been or whether or not she'd played in the attic where we slept. Or had that been her bedroom? I didn't wonder about this other language she spoke, an impenetrable rumble that defined my mother in a different way than her English words and phrases, precise units of sound I could understand, but often didn't want to and had tuned out from an early age.

Only when I was a bit older, in grade five or six, when Mom would sometimes talk about her distant past, dropping a few crumbs about growing up on the farm, only then did I feel it was safe to half-listen. Those crumbs now form a meagre trail pointing in her direction. I know she and her siblings gathered dried manure from the fields for fuel. And that Sam, the eldest, skinned the gophers they caught and sold their pelts. I know that Rachel, the oldest girl, bought caramel corn to put in their stockings one Christmas, that they had a long walk across the fields to get to school, that the girls had to put rags in their panties during their period. I know that Mom—Zina— finished grade twelve, the only sibling to graduate from high school, and then went on to secretarial school, a short distance away in Fair-view, or was it Grande Prairie? Or maybe this higher education, not the high school graduation, was the family first.

Once, remembering parties, Mom's voice brightened and her face opened. And me, too, I opened up with her as she recalled how the men drank vodka and her uncles danced, crouching on the ground and kicking their legs out in front of them, Russian style.

"Like this?" I shouted, fired up with my mother's excitement, crouching down and kicking my own legs out, a boy's step I'd learned in character classes during ballet lessons.

Mom's mouth stretched in a bumpy line across her face and I thought she was going to smile. Then she got her familiar anxious look, and I knew my dancing was getting on her nerves. Clambering up, suddenly graceless, the juice had gone out of my legs, leaving dry, awkward bone.

Over the years, Mom dropped a few crumbs about my grandparents, too. One of my aunts claimed Grandma was the daughter of a mayor: "claimed" was Mom's choice of words, as if the information might not be true. Was that in Ufa, where Palegea was born? Mom said that Grandpa didn't have as "high a standing" as Grandma—those are her words, too, perhaps awkwardly translated from the Russian in which the story had been told to her; I didn't think to ask where he came from or how his parents earned a living. I've no idea how Palegea and Feodor met. Mom only said: "Dad took Mother for a ride in his troi-ka, and refused to bring her back. She had to marry him."

More than once Mom hinted how fierce Feodor could be. "He took things out on Mother," she'd say. He was "old-fashioned," his beard a sign of his Orthodox faith. She'd brighten to add: "Dad was in the Czar's White Army." The hand-tinted photograph in my par-ents' bedroom showed a black-bearded man in leather boots and dark, slim-fitting uniform, a contrast to my mental image of him in white. The Bolsheviks—the Reds Feodor fought against—didn't believe in God, she said. It wasn't until I was a teenager and watched

David Lean's film *Dr. Zhivago* that I first understood a little about
the politics of the Russian Revolution and the ideologies behind the
Communist Reds and Czarist Whites.

Mom saw *Dr. Zhivago* too, when it was shown on television.

"It's a great film!" she said with rare enthusiasm. "That's what it
was like for us!"

When the Russian Revolution began in 1917, Feodor, a small
landowner, was conscripted into the Czar's army. He and Palegea
were living in a Siberian village, Novgorodka, having moved there
from Western Russia soon after their marriage to join family on his
side. In the summer of 1923, with Bolsheviks confiscating land, for-
bidding religious worship and murdering dissenters, they felt they
had no choice but to flee Russia, then called the Union of Soviet
Socialist Republics (though never by my mother's family), along with
several relatives and others from their village. Feodor and Palegea had
four children—Simeon, Raisa, Kapitalina and Natalia—and another
was on the way.

Three days before their departure, my mother, Zinaida, made her
ill-timed entry into the world. This was one event from her past that
Mom told me more than once; each time, her face stretched out loose
and formless as if there was no centre to hold her eyes and cheeks and
mouth together.

"Mother and Dad thought I wouldn't survive the journey, so
they stopped to baptize me."

The baptism was in Blagoveshchensk. From there, they travelled
up the Amur River to the heavily patrolled Chinese border, en route
to Harbin to join a large population of Russians who had arrived
years earlier to work on the Chinese Eastern Railway. These aren't
facts Mom told me; I found them in a family history written by her
cousin. For my mother, the journey was about one intimate moment
hidden in the bottom of a boat crossing into China.

"Mother put her hand over my mouth to muffle my cries."

She said this like it was something she could remember herself,
and only now that she's gone, now that it's too late to ask, only now
do I realize someone must have told her. Palegea? One of her sisters?
Did they use the word "muffle"? Surely it was more than that in a
life-and-death situation requiring the newborn baby make absolutely

no noise. Her mother's hand must have felt heavy and oppressive, even dangerous, stifling any sound that might come gurgling or wailing out of baby Zina's tiny, needy mouth, any sound and any breath, too.

In China, the family lived in a one-room shack, suspended in that small space between two large absences: Mother Russia, who they had abandoned, and Canada, a distant land known only for its promise. Feodor left almost right away for Alberta, where he took on work as a harvester and sold badger skins to earn money for the others' steamship tickets. He wasn't present when Zina began to crawl and to babble—Russian words, of course. Mama, Papa. Soon she was toddling, then talking and walking, then playing mother with a stick she found and cradled like a doll.

Zina was four when Palegea and the five children finally made the ocean voyage. Soon after arriving in Alberta, Zina's "dark and luxuriant hair" was cut off because of lice. That's how Mom described it, though in the one photo I've seen of the family in Harbin, her haircut is short and plain. Yet luxuriant is how she remembered it, and losing her beautiful hair was so devastating that Palegea and Fred (as Feodor had become) bought Zina a bonnet from a catalogue to help her feel better.

In a photograph, Zina peeks out behind her hands, the bonnet a heavy burst of white on top of her head. Behind her and her sisters, an empty clothesline runs the length of the porch; in front of them is the beginning of a fence, a skeleton made up of just the top rung nailed to a few posts. In the middle is a perfectly finished half-open gate, the slats carefully cut to form a graceful arc that suggests there would be finer things to come.

On our last family visit to Hines Creek, just Baba, our grandmother, was alive, though very frail. For weeks before we left, Mom had been on the phone getting updates, her anxious Russian stream of worry and concern overflowing into our home, and she'd been waiting and waiting for Dad's holidays from Lafarge Cement to start. Once we were on the road, Dad drove almost non-stop, grabbing a few hours of sleep overnight at the side of the highway, all six of us camping out in the Parisienne as best we could.

When we finally got to the farm, the car bumped over ruts in the dirt road leading to the house and was engulfed in brown clouds of dust; even with the windows shut, the air felt suffocating. Pulling into the yard, Dad stopped the car abruptly and everyone rushed out. Startled as always by the tall grass, by dragonflies like tiny helicopters, by dry prairie heat, I crossed the yard and entered the house slowly.

It was dark inside, but I could see Baba slumped in her rocking chair. Mom knelt beside her, moaning.

"Get the kids out," Dad said.

I already knew the worst had happened. "If I should die before I wake, I pray the Lord my soul to take." That's what I said every night, on my knees next to my bed, palms pressed together in the hopeful symmetry of prayer hands. It wasn't my grandmother's death that sucked the air out of me, it was my mother's epic moans, upstaging the quiet last breath. In that tableau was a glimpse of baby Zina, who this time would not be muffled.

Of course, this is something I only realize now, as an adult, when the complicated trajectory of time often brings the past into the present right beside me. It shouldn't be possible, but I have become used to the way time and space can suddenly shift. When that scene in the farmhouse returns, as it doubtless will continue to do, my mother's cries carry a whole family history.

Just before Mom entered palliative care at Vancouver General Hospital, we shared our last meal together at a Russian restaurant. My teenage daughter came with us; we chatted until Mom scowled and said, "You two have a lot to say to each other." So we were quiet, listening to Mom air her complaints, mostly about the waitress's slow service. "Oi, where's the food? I'm starving," she kept saying. This time, she really was: her esophageal cancer had advanced to the stage where she could hardly get food down her throat. I only realized how bad it was after our meals arrived: Mom chewed tiny morsels, taking each one out when she thought no one was looking to hide it under a napkin, unable to swallow anything.

We ordered perogies and borscht, some of our favourite Russian food. She'd left Russia so young, yet the country had a hold on Mom and, through her, on me. Russia was always the place where good things came from. Like the uncles' Cossack dance, and the red kerchief Mom sewed for me one summer and called a baboushka. And the piroshky stuffed with hamburger and onion she'd spend all morning making; they always turned out a little heavy and greasy, but I liked them all the same. At Easter, Mom would bake a tall, round loaf of kulich with raisins and candied fruit. She'd greet me on Easter morning with "Khristos Voskrese!" ("Christ is Risen!"). I was supposed to answer "Voistinu Voskrese!" ("Indeed He is Risen!"), but she had never properly coached me, so the ceremony fizzled out, though she'd carry on with the triple kiss.

Baba, baboushka, da, nyet, spaseba, dosvedanya: my vocabulary is minimal. But as a child I loved to hear Mom speaking Russian on vacations at the Alberta farmhouse or when relatives visited us in Vancouver. The thick, dark tangle of her Russian voice was rich and mysterious, not sweet but somehow enticing, like molasses tossed through the air.

That voice and the raging one, too, are within me still. I've come to picture us like a set of Russian nesting dolls: my mother inside me and her mother inside her, in a series of mothers and daughters going endlessly back and back and back. Going forward as well, with me inside my daughter. Though what that means is not my story, but hers.

Curries and Sandwiches

Ishita Aggarwal (India)

My family and I had just immigrated to Canada, and it was my first day of grade one. My parents were nervous about sending me to a new school in a new country, and they compensated in the only way they knew how: I was dressed in the best clothes they could afford, new sneakers and all, and I carried an elaborate lunch in my backpack.

The morning had been uneventful. My classmates weren't particularly friendly, nor were they snide, and I spent most of the first half of the day sitting quietly at my assigned desk. The wall clock ticked away, lunch hour came around, and I assumed it would be as uneventful as everything else. I found a corner away from the hustle and bustle of scurrying children and pulled out one of the few special items my parents had brought from India.

"What's that?" a voice asked.

Startled, I turned and saw a male classmate staring at me. He seemed curious, confused and conflicted all at once.

"My lunch?" I replied, my voice low and somewhat hoarse.

"What's it *in*?" he clarified, "And why does it *smell*?"

I looked down. In front of me sat a metal cylinder composed of four compartments held together by a metal clamp. The two larger compartments contained plain white rice and a few pieces of naan, while the two smaller compartments were filled to the brim with two of my favourite Indian curries. The meal would have been envied and lauded over by my friends back home.

"Th … this is my tiffin," I stuttered.

He snorted, "*Tiffin?* What's a *tiffin?*" He didn't wait for a reply. He turned and walked to a group of boys. He gestured in my direction and I watched as they whispered and winced. I did not eat.

I spent the rest of the day in my head. I had worried about a lot of things when my parents first told me we were moving to a new country. Would my dark skin hinder my ability to make friends? Would I be able to speak as fluently and openly as I was accustomed to? Would I miss my home, my school, my life in India? Not once, however, had I worried about my tiffin or its contents.

That night, my mom asked me why I hadn't eaten lunch. Plucking up my courage, I told her from now on I would either take a "normal" lunch in a "normal" box or no lunch at all. My mom, who was undergoing culture shock of her own, couldn't understand why the food she had packed me was "abnormal." Back home, one's tiffin was a point of pride. An extravagant thali-style meal, featuring an assortment of home-cooked spicy vegetables, dhal, yogurt, pickles and puddings was considered a proclamation of a mother's love. Office-goers everywhere would eagerly await white-capped, dhoti-wearing tiffin wallahs who were in charge of delivering piping hot meals to hundreds of thousands of workers in India's busiest cities.

My mom tried to convince me not to forgo an integral part of my culture for the sole purpose of fitting in. "You'll make friends with or without your tiffin," she promised. I was devastated. I couldn't care less about the cultural significance of my tiffin and, deep down, I knew it would be a lot easier to make friends without it. That night I didn't eat much of my dinner either.

The next day, I felt a sense of impending doom. I stared at the hands of the wall clock, willing them to stop their ticking. But time waits for no one, and lunch hour came around once again. I found a quiet corner, as I had done the day before, and prepared myself for the embarrassment that was soon to follow. Instead, I was pleasantly surprised to find that my mom had packed me a simple sandwich in a basic Tupperware box. Being vegetarian at the time, the traditional egg, chicken and tuna salad sandwiches didn't work for me. In their place, my mom had spent hours in the early morning whipping up a spicy chickpea salad sandwich, something she had never seen nor made before. To this day, I still remember the wave of relief that washed over me upon seeing my "normal" lunch. Never before had I felt so grateful to be ordinary.

A few months ago, while searching for an old book in my basement, I came across my tiffin. Seventeen years older and more experienced, I realized how difficult it must have been for my mom to let go of something she viewed as an important aspect of her identity so I could develop my own. I will never be able to thank her enough for having the foresight to step back, take herself out of the equation and let me adjust to culture shock in the way I felt was right for me.

"Mititei" with a Bilingual Label

DIANA MANOLE (ROMANIA)

I became Romanian only after I emigrated. I was born a member of the country's ethnic majority in Bucharest, the capital city, which was relatively homogeneous. I grew up without thinking of the other ethnic minorities living in Romania, even though the "Other" is considered fundamental in most popular theories of contemporary nationalism. Romania's "imaginary" or perhaps only diverse "imagined" community—in the words of Benedict Anderson—was to me just as distant as the community of Papua New Guinea. To paraphrase Anderson even further, the fact that Vasile, Marioara and I watched the same news program on TV at the same time in Bucharest, Cluj or Iaşi, did not inspire in me a feeling of belonging. Quite the opposite. The aggressive communist propaganda of Ceauşescu's regime kept pressuring us into "loving thy country" and living our lives in the name of a utopian "golden future." At the same time, grocery stores were almost empty, our textbooks and classrooms were flooded with the dictator's pictures and empty promises and we feared that the wrong tone, a political joke or simply a lie told by a secret service (Securitate) informant might send us directly to prison. Being Romanian had become at worst embarrassing and at best irrelevant: "I'm Romanian. So what? I have more important things to think about and other identities to represent me!"

The overly praised two thousand years of Romanian history, surrounded by controversy after the fall of communism, left me disinterested. Even more than that, the idea of historical continuity came directly against the feeling of discontinuity, mainly political, that we felt on a daily basis. I experienced a tiny pang at one point, around 1983, when a tour group from a women's union took me to Sofia. There, a Bulgarian guide marched us in military formation to the train station and showed us the clean platforms and the clocks that actually worked. "Not like in Bucharest!" he said. His chauvinism woke me from the reverie, in which an idyllic Bulgaria smelled like rosewater and strawberry ice cream. In that moment I felt Romanian and was ready to defend my country! And yet, the memory of the North Railway Station (Gara de Nord) in Bucharest, with its floors usually sprinkled with the empty shells of sunflower seeds, the smelly public washrooms with no toilet paper and the overflowing garbage bins, made me swallow my pride and keep quiet. My humiliation over Romania's failure to have public spaces as clean as its southern neighbour faded with time, but a trace of it lingered in my refusal to watch the free and quite entertaining Bulgarian TV shows (la bulgari) as most of my fellow citizens did in a time when Ceauşescu allowed us only two hours of "propaganda" on Romanian Television (TVR, the only television available in Romania during communism). However, to do justice to my former neighbours to the south, *The Barrier* by Bulgarian writer Pavel Vejinov remains one of my favourite novels, and roses often remind me of their country.

It seems that it was fated for train stations and airports to remain closely tied to my sense of national identity. The most important was Otopeni International, where I started walking, or rather, flying down the one-way street that is emigration. A lot of stress, and not a hint of happiness. However, the much-awaited discovery of my new sense of self had begun. Books say it's not the ways in which you are similar to those around you that are significant, but rather the ways in which you are different. In Canada, I was different. "Different how?" you may ask. First, I found out that I was from "Europe," something that had never crossed my mind. Me, along with the French, the Germans and the Italians? Suddenly I felt uplifted to a better category. Pretty soon after, Canadians started placing me in the "Eastern European" crowd. It felt like "home, sweet home." Actually, it made me feel as beautiful as the Polish girls who travelled to Romania during communism, not to enjoy the sun and the Black Sea, but to sell soap, eau de cologne, lipstick, deodorant, nylon blouses, lace panties and other Western luxuries at the illegal flea markets improvised at the nude areas (la solar) on the beach. I felt flattered to have been perceived by Canadians as one of them. My happiness was again short-lived. It seemed I had "Made in Romania" stamped on my forehead, just like cattle wear their owner's initials branded into their behinds. "So? You Romanian?" I would hear more and more often. "Like Tchaushesco, right? And Dracula? Wow! Tell me more about them!"

I changed my wardrobe, makeup, haircut and diet. I took ESL classes to get rid of my accent (little did I know about that not being possible), and I started taking yoga; in short, I did everything I could to get lost in the crowd. In the Canadian crowd. Sometimes, especially if I didn't open my mouth, it worked. During a talkback session after one of the shows of my political parody *The Textile Revolution* in Toronto, when life was good and I felt "integrated," a member of the audience, a *Canadian*-Canadian by his large smile and accent, asked me where I was from. I answered with as much dignity as I could muster, and he started laughing: "Well, now I understand!" I panicked. I felt like I had been discovered and put back in my place. I was silent for the rest of the Q & A. Was it my accent? Or maybe it was the not-so-innocent parody of a revolution in my play that gave me away? I couldn't find it in me to ask.

Step by step, with clarity and a decreasing amount of drama, I accepted my status as an immigrant of Romanian origin, then later as a Romanian-born Canadian, and finally as a Romanian-Canadian. I escaped, after a long time, the feeling of shame that had followed me ever since childhood. I even ate some mititei, a special kind of Romanian sausage, bought from a multi-ethnic European store, together with Borsec mineral water "with bubbles," tripe soup in a jar and even Bulgarian roasted peppers, without any nationalist resentment. Of course, all had the bilingual English-French label that is the standard in Canada. And why lie? I liked what I ate. That's when I decided I was ready to return "home" for the first time since I had emigrated.

In Otopeni, the Bucharest international airport, instead of a greeting, I yelled at my friends, "I'm Romanian!" and they shrugged,

"So? What about it? Did you get your Canadian citizenship?" I had gotten it, but, to their great dismay, it was non-transferable. More unexpected was the fact that once again I had to struggle to blend in. Nothing fit. Not my blonde highlights, gone out of style long ago in Bucharest, or my professional suggestions, which were always cut short: "Where do you think you are? Canada? It doesn't work like that here!" Not even the way I spoke Romanian. It had become "outdated" in less than five years. While I had refused to mix English into my Romanian living in Toronto, my Romanian friends had felt it was more "Western" if they did it in Bucharest. Not even my soap remained unnoticed. "Ah, you smell like Canada. Take me there with you because I'm sick of this place," one of my close friends chattered to me. Then he encouraged all the others to smell me. What could I have told him? I shrugged and gave up reintegrating into my home country, because no matter what I did, an emigrant in sheepskin fools just as few as an immigrant in jeans.

Six

Aileen Santos (The Philippines)

It's 1985. I'm six years old. My father just lost his job. He barricades himself in his room. He's crying. My mom going in only makes it worse. We live in a two-bedroom apartment on Roche Court in a little ghetto in Mississauga. We moved here four years ago from the Philippines. My mom left everything behind.

I remember crying cousins at the airport who I wouldn't see again for another nine years. I remember, even at two years old, proclamations of "I'll never forget you" and "We'll keep in touch." We were family, after all.

I think my dad was the excited one, but now he can't hold down a job. My mom is the only one working consistently. She cleaned toilets, worked at the bank and then finally passed the quiz to work at the post office; it's a permanent job, and it pays well—twenty dollars an hour, a lot for 1985.

I hear Whitney Houston on the radio singing about how bright my future is, how children should always know how beautiful they are inside. But I don't feel beautiful. At school, I am in grade one and I love my teacher, Mrs. Lefebvre, but I'm not really close to any students. L-E-F-E-B-V-R-E. I memorize how to spell her name, and for the longest time, I address her this way. She smells like clean laundry when she hugs me close to her whenever I don't feel well.

There is one dress I feel pretty in—it's yellow with ruffles—and I wear it to school even past the fall weather. My dad fixes my hair into braided ringlets like Princess Leia, and I sit there trying to be patient, but sometimes the pulling and tugging on my scalp hurts. I move and he shoves my head roughly and yells, "Stay still!"

I remember when my mom ran away. My parents had been fighting at a gas station and I sat, invisible at first, in the back seat of our brown Pontiac. They were screaming at each other and I put my hands over my ears, trying to block it all out.

"You see? You're scaring her," he said, blaming her. For a moment, my mother just sat there staring straight ahead until she opened the door—it was a two-door—and I realized she was leaving.

"Don't go! Don't go!" I screamed, getting ready to chase after her. My right leg tried to exit the car, dangling off the side so I could push myself up with my left leg. I was hanging onto the back of her seat for support when she abruptly got out and slammed the door behind her, 150 pounds of steel landing on my skinny right leg. I howled and tried to pull my leg back, but it was stuck. She'd have to come back now; I was injured.

"Mom! Come back!" I screamed hysterically to her fringe-vested back and long black hair, causing others to stare. But she didn't turn around.

My dad had run around to my side of the car, where I was half in and half out. My leg was stuck in the door and tears burned my eyes. Before he crouched down to help me, I heard him yell, "You don't even come back to help your daughter! Look what you did! Putang ina mo!" And he carefully opened the car door and lifted me back in while tears fell like heavy splotches onto my clothing, the weight of it finally hitting me as I sobbed in the back seat. What had I done for her to leave me? What could I have said to fix it? I remember blaming my six-year-old self as my dad silently drove home.

The next day, Mrs. L-E-F-E-B-V-R-E saw my bruised leg as I climbed the stairs to the slide. She called me over, sat me on her lap and asked me kindly, "What happened to your leg?" I shyly buried my head in her armpit, afraid and ashamed to tell her my mom did it.

It wasn't the last time a teacher would question me. Throughout school, I'd be taken aside by caring adults and asked the same three questions:

"What happened?"

"You fell?"

"It was an accident?"

But back in the eighties, they'd sit you directly in front of your parents and ask you in front of them, "Are you parents hurting you?" And you knew better than to give them up because you'd have to go home with them afterward.

My mom came back the next day and all was forgotten, but I never forgot how easy it was for her to walk away—how easy it was for her to leave me.

I wore the yellow dress with ruffles to school in December. My knees shook from how cold it was. I went on the newly formed ice skating rink between the portables, happy to slip and slide on the ice among classmates and older kids at recess. One of them, a boy, pushed me down and I lay there with my underpants showing. People slid around me, and no one helped me up. I was able to get on my freezing-cold hands and knees and crawl to the edge of the ice, where I finally got myself up. We were Roche Court "bus kids," and no one wanted to touch us. They called us Pakis (the derogatory racist term of the eighties, even though we were Filipino) and said we smelled like fish. Parents looked at us in fear. Fear of what, I don't know, but one time I heard a parent say the word lice.

We were clean, even though cockroaches infested the apartment. My stomach always hurt because I was too afraid to go to the bathroom where the roaches would be, either crawling down the drain or just lounging in the toilet. I was too afraid to do my business—number two— and maybe did it once a month, so I was always in the office with an aching belly, wanting my dad to pick me up. It sounds dumb now, but I didn't know back then that you had to poo every day, that it was the norm, that when Mrs. L-E-F-E-B-V-R-E told me to go to the washroom whenever I complained of a stomach ache, that's what she meant. I'd go to the washroom and walk up and down the aisle, kicking open the stall doors. After five minutes, I'd go back to class. She'd come down to my level and whisper, "Is everything okay now?" And because of the way she smiled at me, I'd always say yes.

I don't know why six stands out to me. When telling stories, I always revert back to, "When I was six …" Everything happened at six, even when nothing happened at all.

Six was Roche Court.
Six was Whitney Houston.
Six was Mrs. L-E-F-E-B-V-R-E.
Six was my pretty yellow dress with ruffles.
Six was when my mom left.
And came back.

It's 1985. I'm six years old and my father just lost his job. He barricades himself in his room. He's crying. I fall down at recess. People see my underpants. No one helps me up. I cry. I'm a Roche Court kid and I live with the roaches. My mother never turned around. I blame myself.

Multiverse

Kasia Jaronczyk (Poland)

The key question is not whether the multiverse exists but
rather how many levels it has.
—*Max Tegmark*

I found out my name is Aleksandra Waliszewska and I am a famous artist when I saw one of her paintings on a stiff, perforated card in the centrefold of the Easter issue of *Twój Styl*, a Polish fashion magazine I buy at the EuroFoods deli in Kitchener. In the picture, a woman was lying in bed, partially covered with a blanket, a pale-green pillow under her head. The black-and-white tiled floor led to a small arched window with a view of a hill, a cypress tree and the moon in a phosphorescent blue sky. It looked like a Renaissance painting, but with vigorous, modern brushwork.

I painted that. I could have painted that, I thought. The woman's face was, in fact, the face of Aleksandra, and she was gazing at me questioningly. I stared back. It felt like the three of us—the artist, her recumbent self-portrait and I—were one.

Cholera, nie ma nic, I heard behind me. I turned, the open magazine like a butterfly perched on my hands. My husband had recently increased his Polish vocabulary with the addition of cholera, a swear word (a disease is so much more imaginative than "damn," he'd said). He lifted up a transparent plastic bag with a single limp pączek from the bakery section. *Cholera, nie ma nic.*

What do you mean, there is nothing? I asked.

Only one donut left. I don't even know if it has plum filling, he sighed. And no makowiec! I looked in the box, and it was there. I looked again later, and it was gone.

Schrödinger's cake, I said.

Very funny. He frowned. What am I going to have for dessert?

How about śledziki? I asked with a smirk.

Marinated herring, bleh. He left to browse around the store. I turned back to the painting and the article.

The abstract quantum world contains a vast number of parallel story lines, continuously splitting and merging, but observers can only see a fraction of this full reality.

Back home, I searched the web for more information about the painter. Aleksandra is only a year older than me and she went to the same lycée that I attended for only two months before I immigrated to Canada. Had I stayed in Poland, I would be her. We were both in the same program, one of the first of its kind in the freshly post-communist country—a general stream with an expanded fine arts program. The lycée was named after Cervantes, and it had Spanish instead of the recently obligatory but despised Russian as the foreign-language course.

Aleksandra and I probably had the same teachers, sat in the same rooms. And it is highly likely that she knows all the people from my class. So she is me. She is the me that never happened. I remember-imagine myself, or perhaps her, sitting with a sketchbook at the wide windows that swing open like doors. The windowsill has air bubbles that blister the white oil paint. Or perhaps I sit cross-legged on the herringbone hardwood floor of the hallway. An open box of watercolours on the floor, pad of paper in the lap, paintbrush in hand.

I only have a few memories of that school. A sunny October day when our class decided to go to the Łazienki Park after school. I remember the light, how it lit up the leaves over my head and made them glow like lanterns, and the tall shadow of Jan, a dark-eyed boy who oscillated around me like a dancer. There was also my history teacher, who I had a crush on because he stuttered and had a dimple in his chin that I longed to kiss. He kept calling out my name to answer questions and filled my student record with marks while others had none. Our eyes met and lingered several times. I missed my father—he had been away in Canada for over a year, trying to get us out of Poland. And the bearded art teacher who criticized my work. Van Gogh had trouble with perspective too, I told him. Don't compare yourself to him, he said, as he tossed back my sketch. Why not? I said, and left the room. I had to redo the work several times until he was satisfied.

> *The simplest and most popular cosmological model today predicts that we have a twin in a galaxy about 10 to the 10^{28} meters away; the estimate comes from elementary probability. In fact, there are infinitely many other inhabited planets that have people who look like us, have the same names and memories, and who play out every possible permutation of our life choices.*

In my mind, I still live on that other planet, Poland, as if I had never left. It's my life unlived, or a parallel life—a life I would have had—a life Aleksandra is living. I continuously invent new scenarios. In one of them, I have an affair with the handsome history teacher; he approaches me during recess and runs his hand up my inner arm. I shiver. I was just that type of student, temporarily fatherless, precocious, romantic. This could have happened.

In Poland, I would have finished the visual arts program and continued studying either literature or fine arts like Aleksandra. I've always wanted to be an artist. In my diaries, written since I was six years old, I am tormented by my inability to choose between poetry, prose or art. And by the fact that there isn't enough suffering in my life, even after my hamster died. Emigration changed everything. I thought I would never write in English well enough to be a writer, and I felt pressured to follow a practical career that would lead to a stable job because of what my parents sacrificed to give me "a better future." Had I stayed in Poland, I would have been a painter. I would have been Aleksandra. I am a scientist now.

Many people have regrets about things they did or failed to do, and they imagine what their lives would be like if they had followed an alternate path. But immigrants have left entire lives behind, and existing in a new country seems so unreal—we have never imagined being here, so imagining that we are still in our mother country seems equally possible. This kind of thinking can become a crutch or an excuse. It can also become a source of guilt, especially when something bad happens.

When I was in my early twenties, I was diagnosed with a chronic autoimmune disease that has no known cause. What *is* known is that stress makes it much worse. Stress could possibly cause it, even. At the time, I was more than halfway through my graduate work in a laboratory where the atmosphere had become unbearable— our supervisor was an unprofessional, selfish, abusive woman who pushed us to our limits and exposed us to dangerous chemicals and high levels of radiation. So I blamed the disease on her. And on immigration. I thought if I had stayed in Poland, I would have never been so stressed, I would have never gotten sick. If I had gotten sick in Poland, though, I know I wouldn't have had the quality of health care I have available here. But it is frustrating not to know for sure. And one can wonder about it forever.

> *Quantum mechanics predicts a vast number of parallel universes by broadening the concept of "elsewhere." These universes are located elsewhere, not in ordinary space but in an abstract realm of all possible states. Every conceivable way that the world could be (within the scope of quantum mechanics) corresponds to a different universe.*

The act of making a decision, such as whether or not to emigrate, causes a person to split into multiple copies living in multiple universes.

I left Poland in 1992 when I was fifteen and haven't been back yet for various prosaic reasons: money, health, life events. But now, almost twenty-five years later, I am afraid to go back, because the Poland I remember no longer exists. My Poland is forever a communist country, with food shortages and ration cards, long lines in front of empty stores, vacant streets and parking lots, playgrounds on construction sites and the rare, precious joys of oranges, bananas, blue jeans and Barbie dolls. Poland now is like any other Central European country; the fashions, food, stores, people and their preoccupations are international.

My Polish friends are in their forties and have families and adult problems. But since, according to quantum mechanics, all possible states exist at every instant, and since the passage of time may be in the eye of the beholder, we are all fifteen years old in one of my multiverses. We are all in grade eight. I have a huge crush on A. He has grown a chest and wide shoulders overnight—like Trip Fontaine from *Virgin Suicides*. He has bad acne, curly hair and eyes like bitter chocolate. He keeps looking over his shoulder at me across the classroom and smiling. I forget my gym uniform on purpose to read the Polish Romantic poets instead of playing volleyball, and I imagine A in a tailcoat, a high-neck collar and a top hat. A stylish cravat around his Adam's apple. When I look up from my book, I see A sitting against the wall across the hallway staring at me. I pretend to read, and glance over the pages to check if he is still there. My heart thumps so loud he must hear it. When he comes over, the tips of our sneakers touch and I feel faint. I make an excuse and leave, wishing I had stayed.

In the summer, he sends me a postcard with a picture of a seaside sunset and a note that says, "Greetings from the Baltic, cheers, A." I cry myself to sleep because of that "cheers," and I suspect that his mother, who is friends with mine, made him write the postcard. Unfortunately, he seems to be in love with K, a girl with freckles and a flat nose, who for some inexplicable reason is very popular. She is the first one of us to get her period—she wore a pad for several days each month to make it come. Years later, I look at her in an old class photo. She has beautiful, womanly breasts, whereas I, with my short hair and flat chest, look like A's younger brother.

A saw me off at the airport. My mother was turned away from us, bent over our luggage, reshuffling pots and books from one valise to another because some were over the weight limit. I was too shy to do anything other than shake his hand. He grabbed me in his arms and gave me a hug. He smelled like caramelized onions and pine cones.

Throughout my life I've thought of that moment and wished I had acted differently. This is the spot where the random quantum processes cause the universe to branch into multiple copies, one for each possible outcome. My alter-ego on another quantum branch runs her hands over his wide back and kisses him passionately on the mouth. In this universe, time stands still, and our kiss is infinite.

During my first three years in Canada, I thought of A constantly. There were other boys who caught my eye: Julius, who had long hair and played the violin; the wide-backed blond who always opened doors for me, and who I later found out was also Polish; the tall, slim Ethiopian who kissed my hand when we were introduced, as was the Polish custom. But none of them compared to A. In this universe, we were light years apart. In another universe, we are a couple, we are dating, then living together. We get married and have children. In this universe, I dreamt about him incessantly. In my dreams, he was often unhappily married to someone else, but hesitated to divorce her because they had little children. He asked me for advice and I hesitated. When I woke up I was always mad at myself that I couldn't strip my morality and let my nakedness sway him.

In my late teens I was convinced I would not be able to marry another man until I went back to Poland and saw A. But time passes. I am happily married and have lovely children here in Canada. And I am always planning to visit Poland. I know that once there, I will think: "I remember this, I remember doing this, I remember being here," but I also will always think, "this is where I would have gone, this is what I would have done, this is who I would have been had I stayed in Poland."

It is a comforting thought, that I have several lives in parallel, that while I chose to live here in Canada, somewhere in the multiverse—though the laws of quantum physics make it impossible for me to perceive—I am also still living my life in Poland.

One day I reconnected with A on the Internet and he told me his wife had an affair and a child with another man, and that he was considering a divorce. I don't know if I love her or just pity her, he said. A spot opened up for me in his world. The world I split from years ago when I emigrated. The entire architecture of my parallel world, my possible other existence, is already in place. I don't need to invent it; it exists even though I am not there. All I would need is to be plucked out of this life, as if by the hand of a god, and be dropped back into the other universe.

I told A he probably feels both, and that he should give her another chance. Another life. It's what all of us want, after all. Even the physicists.

All citations come from Max Tegmark, "Parallel Universes," *Scientific American*, May 2003.

My Father's Duality

Nam Kiwanuka (Uganda)

Our car was racing through the streets of Kampala, Uganda, with my father at the wheel, a friend of his in the passenger seat and my older sister and I huddled together in the back seat without seat belts. There was a rusted hole in the bottom of the car and we could see the road flashing by as we sped away. The car was also missing its doors. I had a smile on my face. I'd never felt safer.

As a child in Uganda, I used to brag about my father. At school I would boast that he was the strongest dad around and he could do more push-ups than any other dad. Plus he always did them on his knuckles! I would mimic his martial arts moves and whenever he would leave, I would beg to go with him. I never wanted to be apart from him.

But a few years later, after we moved to Canada, at the age of thirteen I tried to kill myself just to get away from him.

In Uganda my father was the one person I could count on. I was around five or six years old when our mother left us. My dad became a twenty-something single dad with four children. It wouldn't have surprised anyone had he left as well, but he chose to stay with us when we were the most vulnerable. We lived with him and his friends who eventually became my uncles. My father was the provider and my uncles became our teachers. My dad would disappear for weeks at a time, and when he came back he would have money. I don't know where or how he made the money, but we had money for food, for school fees, and on rare occasions he would bring second-hand clothes that my auntie's children had outgrown. At one point we lived in a three-room shack with an outdoor toilet. There were nights when it was difficult to fall asleep because of the rat-a-tat-tat sound of gunshots in the distance, but those are some of the happiest memories of my childhood.

Because of the civil war, we eventually fled Uganda. Along with my father and uncle, my siblings and I walked from Kampala to the Kenyan border. We lived in a refugee camp until a woman from London, Ontario, called Sidney Tebbutt, sponsored us to Canada with the help of her church.

The change in my dad was gradual. We had been living in Canada for over a year when my dad's sponsorship of his girlfriend in Uganda came through. She would become my stepmother and she was also the mother of my half-sister and stepbrother. I don't know if it was the added responsibility of taking care of a larger family, or because of missing Uganda, or because he had post-traumatic stress disorder, but my dad's personality changed. I often say that I had two fathers: the one in East Africa that I was completely devoted to and loved more than anything, and the one in Canada who replaced him.

In Canada, when my dad came home each day, we were required to welcome him. My sisters and I would kneel, as is the Ugandan tradition. Even if I wanted to, there was no way of avoiding him. Soon after arriving home, he would scan the house to see what was out of place. On one occasion, my sister had placed the shower curtain on the wrong side of the tub. My father began to yell and shoved one of my other siblings. I ran in to intervene and he slapped me.

Eventually the beatings became a part of my life. To this day, I still think about the beatings but also his verbal abuse. He called me a slut. He said I would never amount to anything, that I was a burden; we were all burdens. Once he grabbed me around the neck and slammed my head against the wall, leaving a hole in the drywall. He would repeatedly send me to bed without dinner. At school the teachers would ask me about the bruises on my face. I lied. "I fell down," I said. "My siblings and I were playing." No one asked me to lie but a part of me knew that I needed to protect my father.

I often think about what changed in my dad. Life had always been difficult in Uganda and later Kenya, but he had never been violent toward me. Yes, I had been disciplined, but there was an unwritten code of discipline where children were only hit below the waist. It sounds absurd, but it's how things were done in our community. I suppose the idea was that you showed restraint in that you were trying to teach your child something as opposed to taking out your frustrations on them.

It seemed easier for my stepmother to settle into life in Canada. She had access to computer training programs and support groups for immigrant women. My father didn't. He had to figure out this new way of life on his own. He had been raised in a patriarchal society where men were kings, and now he was living in a society that taught his daughters that they were equal to men, and his wife was learning how to use computers. When he left his house, the outside world called him the n-word and his identity was now a caricature of a stereotype.

Although granny, the woman who sponsored us, tried to help as much as she could, it was probably difficult for my dad to connect with her or for her to identify with him. While my father had been a drinker when we lived in East Africa, he became more dependent on alcohol and it was common for him to come home late at night drunk. When he was in that state he would turn up his stereo and the music would jolt us from our sleep. He would listen to the music at a volume that shook the house until the next morning.

A few years after my suicide attempt, my sisters and I came home from the movies. It was a frigid December night. Our nightly curfew was six o'clock, but this time we rebelled and came home at ten. We had phoned our stepmother to tell her we were running late, but when we tried to open the door, my father had locked us out. The hour that followed is too painful to recount, but the police were called. My older sister and I worked out a deal with our father so that he wouldn't be jailed. He wanted us to move out. I was sixteen at the time and my sister was eighteen. We agreed to move on the condition that he promise to change and that he wouldn't beat our siblings anymore. So we left and the charges against him were never filed.

I am now a mother of two young children. I often think about what would have happened to me and my siblings had our dad left when our mother did. I still carry the scars of those years, but somehow, someway, we survived. For that, in spite of what my father did to me, I am forever grateful to him.

Catalyst

JAMELIE BACHAALANI (LEBANON)

The LRT comes to a sudden halt. The driver's static voice blares over the intercom like Big Brother—there will be a brief delay before we start up again. I am shaken from my sleepy daze. My head is leaning on the window, my eyes struggling to adjust to the sunlight. The scenery between Clareview and Churchill, before the ground opens up and consumes us, is nothing but partially boarded-up buildings and empty fields covered in snow. Sometimes in the spring you can see the hidden camps of people who linger briefly, then disappear. I suppose, in a way, the prairies have their own beauty—one of bleakness and space. I stare at the apartment buildings in the distance, the shades of brown matching the dirt and bare trees, and think of my father's brown, wrinkled skin. I imagine him staring out the window of our third-floor apartment, his hands behind his back twirling a misbaha and whispering curses in broken English about the cold and the cement.

"This goddamn province," he exclaims, throwing his hands into the air before sulking off to the living room. After forty years, a marriage and five children, he still spits on this country.

ooooo

On Sunday mornings, I wake up to my father singing church hymns in his loud, growling voice. When I was younger, he reminded me of a bear waking up from hibernation, but now I stand three inches taller than him. Unable to fall back asleep, I crawl out of my bed to join him in the living room.

"Jamelie! Come look," he screams at me from behind his computer, forgetting he still has his headphones in. He's always screaming at me to come look at something. Most of the time it's a black and white music video in a language I can't understand, so I just smile and nod. Sometimes he translates articles from Arabic to English for me, but I can never appreciate his enthusiasm. Instead, I push the guilt of losing the ability to speak in my father's native tongue deep down.

"Look. This is Kab Elias. This is my village." He taps his fingers hard against the computer screen. With the excitement of a child, he points to pictures of white houses with orange roofs surrounded by mountains. The Mount Lebanon range extends along the entire country and the Mediterranean coast. When I was a teenager, I used to imagine Lebanon as an endless desert, nothing but a thick layer of sand for miles and miles, and a smug smirk would spread across my face when my father compared his home to mine. As if anything could compare to Lebanon.

"Did it ever snow in your town?"

"Sometimes. But not like here. You can't even leave your house here!" And then he is gone on a tangent, mixing his English with Arabic until it's indecipherable.

But Kab Elias is a city now. The third-largest city in the Beqaa Valley. The land my father is from no longer exists the way he remembers it, and his Kab Elias is a place I will never know. I imagine him as a loud-mouthed farm boy smoking a cigarette and walking down the street alleys to the market with his pet lamb.

"You have to believe me," is how he usually starts off every story. "She sat right on my shoulder the whole way there."

I was twenty the first time he told me about his pet lamb and his family's farm, and I wonder how many secrets, how many stories, he'll take to his grave.

ooooo

"If he loves Lebanon so much, why doesn't he ever visit?" Joseph, my oldest brother, asks from the driver's seat of the car. He is clenching the steering wheel so tightly the skin over his knuckles is turning white. We're lost somewhere just off Whyte Avenue in search of the antique mall. We only have an hour before it closes.

"Displaced immigrants rarely ever go back. He was forced to leave," my brother Assaad, three years younger than Joseph, answers back. Assaad is visiting from Vancouver, and most of his time has been spent sitting at my father's side showing him black and white music videos in a language I can't understand.

"But Mom always told me his family needed money so they sent him here to work." My voice wedges in between the two of them from the passenger seat.

"We can never know for sure, but there was a civil war. Look up the bus massacre," Assaad tells us, but Joseph isn't listening. To him, Lebanon is a place that might as well not exist.

But a war would explain why my father sometimes calls out for his own father in his sleep; it would explain the three bottles of anti-depressants on his nightstand, and why he's often awake at 3:00 a.m., staring at the latest news updates from Beirut, crying.

ooooo

The screen of my iPhone lights up, telling me I have a new Facebook message. I click on the notification.

"Hello, I'm Ralph. Your uncle's son. Your uncle's name is Maurice; ask your dad about his brother. We are in Lebanon. Your grandmother's name is Jamelie, and your grandfather's name is George. Sorry, I can't spell English well."

I read Ralph's message three times and try to form a reply in my head. I scroll through photos of him with his father and siblings. Ralph is fifteen. His older brother is a priest. All of them still live in Kab Elias, and I wonder why my uncle never left like my father did. But those are things we don't discuss, so I'll never know.

"Hi, Ralph. My dad has mentioned Maurice before. Your English is fine."

"Can you please send us a photo of my uncle? I wish I could meet him."

"Of course. Just wait until I'm done at school."

My father is concentrating on his online poker match when I

tell him Maurice's son messaged me and wants a picture of his uncle. A smile spreads across his face.

"Take a picture of me with Winry."

He poses in his computer chair with the family cat, an overweight gray Persian, and tells me to keep messaging Ralph. I send the pictures and a few replies before I stop writing back, but I tell myself it's okay because one day maybe I'll meet him and his father and his siblings.

ooooo

I sit down at the kitchen table, open my laptop and search up "bus massacre Lebanon." I survey the links, clicking through Wikipedia, BBC News and *The New York Times*, trying to absorb all the information.

> *On April 13, 1975, Palestinian guerrillas reportedly opened fire on the congregation outside a Maronite Christian Church.*

My father is across from me in the living room, watching the news on his computer, his headphones plugged in. For a brief second it crosses my mind to ask him about it, but the Lebanese don't talk about the war, or at least that's what Assaad says. So instead I focus my attention back on the article.

> *In the commotion that followed, armed Phalangist militiamen took to the streets and began to set up roadblocks. Shortly after mid-day, a bus carrying Palestinian refugees drove through the streets where an armed Phalangist presence waited.*

I imagine him, only twenty-six at the time, with his slicked-back hair and bellbottoms, packing his belongings into a single suitcase along with a vow to never return. My father told me about his dream to become a priest at the church in his village, but instead he was forced to give it all up to work as a plumber in a province that mocks the way English words trip over his tongue.

There is a photo of the bus in the BBC News article. It is much smaller than I imagined. My cursor blinks beside a new paragraph:

Upon seeing the bus pass by, the Christian militiamen opened fire on the bus, killing 17 passengers. This bloodshed was the spark that erupted the 15-year-long civil war in Lebanon that led to more than 150,000 people dead and even more injured, or forced to emigrate.

I see him crying beneath the orange-tiled roof as he says good-bye to his family before boarding his plan to Limassol, Greece, where he waits six months to receive clearance to enter Canada. Six years later, the Shatila Massacre claims almost thirty-five hundred lives across Beirut in only two days. The massacre was a retaliation for the assassination of newly elected Lebanese president Bachir Gemayel. I google his name. Images of a handsome man speaking into a micro-phone, or standing in front of the Lebanese flag, pop up. One of the photos I already know; it's the same black and white photo my father keeps on his desk.

ooooo

My dad and mom cram two coolers, six backpacks and five tired chil-dren into their beat-up white Ford van. It is seven in the morning. We should reach Banff a little after one. I bring a pile of books; I am convinced I can read all of them in just four hours while my sister uses me as a headrest, her sweaty skin sticking to my own bare legs. I manage only a few chapters of *Goosebumps* before I drift off too. My dad wakes us up when we reach the mountains. My small body is overwhelmed by the rock giants looming over us, a feeling that will never fade.

"Ha! Look at the waterfall." He points at a mountain farther away with a barely noticeable stream of water trickling down it. "You'll never see one like the one in my town. We would go swim-ming and jump off the cliffs. All day you would swim."

His favourite part of the trip is the mountain goats. The van curves with the highway, a wall of rock emerges on our left and we see the animals climbing. My dad pulls over and ushers us all out of the van to take in the sight.

"Look how they climb straight up without falling." He watches them with binoculars as my mother documents it all with her camera.

"Do you have mountains in Lebanon?" I ask my father, unaware that the only reason we come here is because it makes him feel, for a moment, like he is in Kab Elias again, surrounded by mountains.

We'll Walk

Nadine Bachan (Trinidad)

You are a toddler. Everyone still lives in Trinidad. I am not born yet.

Our sister is less than a year younger than you, and you're often mistaken for twins. But she begins to run and jump, and you drag yourself forward with your elbows on the floor. Everyone carries you in their arms.

One doctor devastates our parents when he tells them that you are likely to be severely disabled, both physically and mentally. He says not only will you never walk, but you will also never talk, read or write. He says you will need constant care. Life will be very hard for you, with you.

You and our sister are inseparable. When she begins to talk, so do you. When she begins to read, so do you. You're growing and learning like every other child, a marvel against all that's been predicted, which makes our parents wonder how much more you can do or become.

Dad takes you to SickKids Hospital in Toronto for medical tests. Doctors there offer hope when they tell him that your cognitive functions aren't impaired. They also assert that you will always be disabled. Before Dad takes you back to Trinidad, the doctors recommend two things: (1) get you a wheelchair as soon as possible, and (2) consider moving to Canada.

A pious relative convinces our parents to take you to her church for the miracle cure. After several sermons and a donation large enough to feed the congregation, the reverend presses his sweaty palm upon Dad's head, attempting to strike the devil from the father to cleanse the son. Dad locks his legs straight and refuses to fall to the ground.

Mom keeps going, keeps hoping, and takes you to a large revivalist gathering where you are too young to understand as the enfeebled stand, dance and shout praises to the Lord. An assistant to the preacher looks at you, then at Mom, and says, "He's still not ready to be healed. Come back next time, and bring more money."

That night, our parents finally see eye to eye when it comes to hoping for the divine remedy: never again.

∞∞∞

When you are five years old, our grandparents return from a month-long trip across Europe with a gift found in an English hospital for you: a wheelchair. You cry and climb back down to the ground every chance you get, but soon settle into this new position. Mom and Dad, too, eventually adapt.

One of our uncles gives you the nickname Wheels, a moniker that's stuck with you to this day. He takes you every day to the only school in the country for children with disabilities, an hour drive each way from San Fernando to Port of Spain. Before long, our parents find out that you aren't getting an education there. The school functions as little more than a daycare.

As they seek to find an appropriate school for you, our parents create homeschooling plans. Our sister and our cousins go to the local primary school in their blue uniforms while you stay at our grandparents' house, where you are much happier helping our grandmother with the cooking and gardening than completing your prepared lessons.

There is no proper school for you in Trinidad. When our parents go to the Canadian Consulate General to collect the necessary forms, an official informs them, off the record, that they will need to obtain detailed proof that you won't be a burden on resources. He asks blankly, in an official tone that holds neither discrimination nor malice, "Why should we accept someone like that in Canada?"

When our parents are unable to answer, he gives them a book on Canadian civics and government, tells them to make sure they know as much as they can.

"If we're qualified, we'll get in," Dad assures Mom. "We'll try our best."

No one wants us to leave. The uncle who used to drive you to school builds his home flat so you at least have one place that's easy to visit. Everyone assures our parents that they will always be around to help you. Our grandfather tells our parents not to leave the good jobs they worked so hard to gain. With heavy hearts, our parents begin the application process.

Dad takes you to Toronto for more tests and to receive the official medical report that proves your paraplegia to be permanent but stable, and your mental capacities to be normal. Meanwhile, Mom works on an education study entitled "Educating the Physically Disabled in Trinidad and Tobago" for the University of West Indies.

Dad's skills from working in Trinidad's oil industry make him highly employable in Canada and therefore a favourable candidate. The two-year application process, though gruelling and intensive, is positive overall and provides enough of an encouraging push for both our parents to resign from their jobs—letting go of their benefits, pensions and the future they thought they would have in Trinidad—and prepare themselves as best as possible for a path unknown toward the possibility of a good life for you.

ooooo

On November 13, 1988, I'm crying. At three years old, I've just experienced my first plane ride and we've landed in a strange new place that's oh so cold. Dad meets us at the airport with hugs and kisses, his arms full of coats, scarves and gloves for us, then takes us to our first Canadian home—an apartment in a huge high-rise building in the suburbs of Rexdale.

Dad works overtime, while it takes Mom over a year to find permanent work teaching high school science. On the day we are registered as permanent residents of Canada, a particularly compassionate officer ensures we receive health insurance right away, waiving the three-month waiting period.

Family and friends are here. Family and friends have made their way to us, have moved from Trinidad to offer close support. Family and friends are made in the good people our parents meet as they struggle to find work, support and common ground. Joviality sweeps through our lives as we find reasons to celebrate and be together as often as possible. Community forms around us like a soft, warm shell.

ooooo

For as long as I can remember, you use the term "walk."

ooooo

Our first house—one of several bungalows shaded by towering maple trees—becomes known as the one with the really mean cat and the big green ramp. We live across the street from an accessible school but you're not allowed to walk the two minutes it takes to get there with our sister and me. Rain, snow or shine, you have to ride the short bus every morning and every afternoon. The student-support staff and the school board are clear about this particular mandate: safety comes first. After all, the neighbourhood is rife with all kinds of insurmountable obstacles for you—from slightly uneven sidewalks to the gentle, asphalt-paved slope that leads up to the schoolyard.

You like to sleep in, making the bus driver wait. You like to hang out with your friends after the dismissal bell rings, making the bus driver wait.

Our first visit back to Trinidad occurs when I am six years old. I am introduced to countless people that you, our sister and our parents know. Family. They hold us tightly when we arrive. I don't remember them but I love them all immediately. Our voices mimic the singsong tones of everyone around us. I watch as you, most of all, are enfolded in love and awe. Life in Canada has done wonders. Your light shines for all to see and our parents beam with a joy I have not seen before. This homecoming is glorious.

When I blink, the weeks have come and gone, and we are being told to say goodbye to a sea of tear-streaked faces. They weep like they're in mourning. Our grandparents look down on us briefly from the balcony of their home before disappearing inside.

It will be years before we return.

Five years after that first cold day in Canada, we stand in a room full of people to sing the national anthem and recite the Oath of Citizenship. We pose for a photograph alongside the presiding judge and a member of the Royal Canadian Mounted Police. Our sister, mother and I have donned dresses. You and Dad are wearing suits. Your tie is covered with the characters from the *Looney Tunes*.

Some family members who came with us in the early days eventually move back to Trinidad, including a cousin who lived with us for several years and bonded with us like a brother. His leaving must have been harder on you than you have ever told us.

Telephone calls to and from Trinidad are short in duration. Voices are delayed and heavy with emotion while wishing us a Merry Christmas or Happy New Year. Mom and Dad are both happy and sad during the holidays, at Easter, in the winters, day by day.

We write and receive handwritten summaries of life. My left handed chicken scratch begins every letter the same:

How are you? I am fine. I got all As in school . . .

Our grandmother, in careful cursive, ends her letters the same:

God bless and keep you.

She writes her last letters to us when I am eleven years old.

ooooo

You and our sister graduate from middle school, then high school. I'm bringing up the rear, always five years behind. As the years pass, less and less of me yearns for the experience of Trinidad. The longing is a dull and subtle pang that everything near and immediate piles upon. Living in Canada, and only truly knowing myself as Canadian, buries it. The recollections of the few visits there when I was young have transformed into delicate nostalgia, best left forever hazy and dream-like.

I can understand why Trinidad constantly pulls you and our parents back. It's in what you have that I do not: the unbreakable bond that forms when you remember a place as home. I realize that feeds the frustration you and our parents feel knowing that Trinidad makes no strides in becoming more accessible or accommodating to the disabled.

ooooo

We carry on here. There is so much to do.

ooooo

While completing your undergraduate degree at Ryerson, you take public transit and often miss class when buses arrive at your stop with either broken ramps or drivers who have no idea how to operate them. I half joke with our sister about getting the local news to do a human-interest segment. Instead, our parents buy you your first car.

You frequent the nearby pub with your university friends so often that the owners eventually install a ramp. One evening, our sister and her friend accompany you and watch from the bar as you get nicely buzzed and end up in the middle of the dance floor, surrounded by women. I hear the story from our sister the next day while you nurse your hangover, lying in bed with the covers over your head, our parents pretending they're none the wiser.

We all want to see a show at the theatre downtown. Our sister goes online, looks up wheelchair seating. There is none. She calls the box office and is told that there actually is an accessible seat, but the person will have to get out of the wheelchair to get to it. The man on the phone asks if this can be done.

You lift weights. You swim. You dismantle your wheelchair and place its pieces into the back seat of your car whenever you head to work, or do errands, or go on road trips. So, yeah, you can get to that theatre seat. But our sister doesn't divulge that. You know how she gets. Instead, she spits into the phone, "This is ridiculous," and hangs up.

Just because you can doesn't mean this is okay.

ooooo

I've asked you to pick me up from the passenger kiss-and-ride at the subway station. You're frequently late when it comes to things like this. How you drive your RX8 like a speed demon and yet never arrive anywhere on time will always be a mystery to me. While I wait, a car pulls into one of the two wheelchair parking spots in the round-about, and I immediately see red because there is no blue permit on the car's dashboard or licence plate.

I approach when a young man walks up to the car and opens the passenger door. I say, "Um, you're not supposed to park here. This is an accessible spot." The young man looks at me half-ashamed, but the driver tells me to mind my own business. As I stutter out noises of offense, he shouts at me to shut up, pulls his passenger all the way into the car and peels off.

When you arrive, I tell you about this travesty, shaking and wiping my eyes. You nod, driving us back toward the main road, and dismiss it gently by changing the subject to where we might grab a bite to eat.

Mom and Dad take turns being angry about people's ignorance when it comes to disability and accessibility issues. They also take turns shushing each other about the correct time, place and company in which to be indignant.

I listen while someone tells them, "Not every parent has it in them to do what you've done." Mom nods with a shrug. Dad sits back in his chair and exhales softly. Neither one thinks they've done anything extraordinary.

As you make your way across the stage to receive your Bachelor of Science degree, the entire auditorium applauds you. Our parents cry large, shuddering tears. Our sister and I are quieter, but our faces are streaked all the same.

Your girlfriend laughs at the huge graduation photo that's eventually mounted on the wall in our parents' living room. You've been seeing her for several months now. She fits right in with all of us.

"You look so serious," she says through giggles. It's true: you're like a bull without horns. So stern, so unlike you.

ooooo

Dad reads the online Trinidad news this morning and sees a video that's causing some buzz, titled "POLICE BRUTALITY AGAINST MAN

IN WHEEL CHAIR IN TRINIDAD," and now he's stressed because you're currently visiting Trinidad and, gosh, what are the odds? The man in the video is not you, but Dad is no less incensed. I listen to him opine philosophically and politically about Trinidad's state of affairs, transitioning from outrage to nostalgia and back, as he reflects with sadness in his voice on how little has changed in the last thirty years.

You've visited Trinidad much more than I have. You're there for the weddings, for the festivities, for the comradery of all those who welcome you with open arms, no matter how much time passes. There are always people to cart you up and down stairs, to push you through the sandy beaches, to make sure you're as comfortable as possible and that you're entertained. The greatness of the love that reaches out to you is like none other.

ooooo

You and I head to the Annex in downtown Toronto, where our sister lives now. The three of us have sushi. You treat, making a joke about me and her being broke students. Afterwards, we go for coffee. A man sitting alone sees us come in and gets up so quickly that the book he's reading thuds to the floor.

"You guys can have this table," he says, pulling one of the chairs away.

You thank him, then head over to the counter to buy our drinks and flirt with the barista. For an hour, we laugh and tease each other with inside jokes, then realize that the café's washroom door is too narrow for your wheelchair to fit through.

Later, our sister and I lean against the trunk of your car, looking out at the sidewalk traffic, while you urinate into a water bottle and then empty it down the sewer drain.

ooooo

When Mom and Dad retire, they tell us they want to spend more time in Trinidad. Over several months, they completely remodel the main floor of the house of our grandparents, both of whom have long since been laid to rest. Once finished, the two-bedroom space is completely accessible. Along with our uncle's house, which is still flat, it's one of the very few places you get around in without assistance.

Our parents have lived two lifetimes. One in Trinidad, and then one in Canada. I hope, just as you and our sister hope, that they will now experience only the best of both worlds. They have earned their paradise in more ways than I can recount.

I find the study our mother completed before we moved to Canada. The pages are nearly three decades old, the typewritten words faded. In the acknowledgements, she thanks our father as well as several colleagues and family members who supported her throughout the process. She quotes from an old song:

> *See what we've got deep inside*
> *Don't just see our imperfections*
> *But the courage in our stride*
>
> *We are not to be discarded*
> *From our society*
> *When our goals are set before us*
> *We challenge them daringly*

The dedication is simple: *To my son.*

You are a man who will always seem young at heart. Everyone lives everywhere. Trinidad, Canada, the United States, the United Kingdom. I am in Vancouver now. Twice a year, I visit you, our sister and our parents. Skype, text messages and emails keep everyone connected. The distance doesn't feel as precious as it once did.

Your girlfriend points out the lake and the boardwalk as we stare out the window of her apartment. Today, summer is reaching its peak, and the lake winks at us from afar.

"Let's go for a walk," you say.

We wander slowly, having the kind of conversation we will forget once it's finished. There are moments of easy silence as we take in the balmy afternoon.

Recently, Trinidad has found its way back to the forefront of my mind. Thoughts on life and kin there creep into my writing, into quests for anecdotes from our parents, into my understanding of myself. I am curious, open to what I could learn now. I wonder if I should plan a trip. I wonder when you'll visit Trinidad again, when you might be able to find time. You have a home to upkeep, a career, and friends who are always taking you out and about. Your life here has been so very full.

Our sister pushes your wheelchair while you and your girlfriend hold hands. I fall behind a little to observe. All around us children scamper. Babies watch the world from strollers—little ones who will soon run with abandon.

Previously published in *Hazlitt*, in October 2015

How to Emerge from the Belly of the Whale

Sarah Munawar (Pakistan)

Arabic: لاَ إِلَهَ إِلاَّ أَنتَ سُبْحَـٰنَكَ إِنِّي كُنتُ مِنَ الظَّـٰلِمِين

Transliteration: Laa ilaaha ilaa anta Subhaanaka innee kuntu minaz-
zaalimeen

Translation: "There are none worthy of worship besides You. Glori-
fied are You. Surely I am from the wrongdoers." (21:87)

I cannot remember exactly when but at some point between immigrating and living here for seventeen years, what I was taught of Allah,
Qiyamat, Jannat, Dua in Lahore was erased. Tales of prophets per-
forming miracles and embodying (extra)ordinary piety passed from
one generation to another, and then to me, where they became faint
whispers. What were once as important as the Alif, Ba, in Pakistan,
the reasons why I did not steal, did not lie, became truths from some
distant time, forgotten, dismembered from me. My parents tried their
best to honour their duty; they sent me to Sunday Islamic school on
cold Ontario mornings, told me stories of strong women in Islam like
Hazrat Aisha, taught me Sura Fatiha every time I forgot it, but even
their most sincere efforts could not stop the long march of history
toward the secular. All that remained on my tongue was the Sha-
hada: that there is one God and the Prophet Muhammad (peace be
upon him) was his messenger. Beyond this, I was no longer sure if the

men in those stories ever existed, if such miraculous things actually happened in the past. Whether it was growing up in Ontario's public school system, or the fear of being typecast as a terrorist after 9/11, or the "God is Dead" introduction to philosophy in first year, the Islamic ways of being, seeing, eating, knowing were no longer close to me.

Religion became a truth from some distant time buried under the tongues of self-righteous aunties, and mullahs and political leaders who used Allah as an instrument of power. In my imagination, my relationship to Islam, to Allah, was as near and far as the smells, sounds, smiles and sorrows of home and my family in Pakistan. Growing up as a child in Lahore, whenever I thought of Allah, an image of Jinnah would present itself in my mind. I never understood why; maybe it was the nationalist propaganda at school, or maybe it was just an innocent conflation of State with God as a child. And with every year that passed in Canada, Allah as well as Jinnah became dispossessed from my memory, my mind and my body. Sometimes, when eating an imported chaunsa, smelling the ever-present scent of dye in shalwar kameez or seeing my mother laugh like my nanoo, I feel parts of me thawing and I feel close to Allah again, to home again. I feel like myself again, before I began to play pretend. The nostalgia of home has always been a vessel outside of time where I found Allah without fail. But the more winters I spent here, the harder it was to find my way back home to Allah.

Or so I thought until one fateful morning. Though I had learned how to read the Quran and how to perform Salat in Lahore, it was in a cold, Canadian hospital that I finally understood how to truly pray. At twenty-one years old, I witnessed my first miracle.

I will never forget the day some white man in a white coat in a white room asked my mother to make a decision to let my father live or to let him go. I do not remember what made me feel more powerless: the invisible shadows of empire, the last word of science or the inevitability of death. It was then I learned that stories, our ideas and beliefs of who counts as a human being, a life worth living, could kill someone. Who was this man? Where did his authority come from? And on this pale blue dot floating in space, where was the Allah we prayed to? And more than anything, where did my Abu Jaan go?

This is where my story begins. The smell of sanitized hands, the hollow coo of diagnostics, the deafening silence with which grief fills up a room, cling to my body like a phantom limb. This is a story that cannot be rewritten, a truth that cannot be wrung dry of the sacred, a story based on true events.

Somewhere, near all of us, there is a place where life begins and ends. It is also a place of endless waiting, of prolonged suffering. There is an extraordinary, almost fantastical emptiness sealed within the four white walls of hospital quiet rooms. A place where the language of what is tangible, measurable and rational prevails over the secret and unseen metaphysics of sentience, of attachment, of the beyond. A place where you became hyper-aware of earthly time, every second, but forget what day it is and how long you've been there for.

With a disturbing ease, Dr. Healey revealed to us our father's fate: "The time for miracles and faith is over and the time to make a decision is now. Your father is in a coma and with the extent of anoxic brain injury from the cardiac arrest and the blockage from the double stroke, he will most likely not survive the night."

The tasbihs on the table, the Quran, the prayers, nothing had worked, nothing made sense after we heard these words. Nothing, nothing, nothing, it was as if he had single-handedly taken everything from us, our father, our world, our language, our religion. But what about that white light my brother saw in the basement the night before? And that dove we saw on our way to the hospital? It must have been a pigeon. And what of the vision my mother had in a spell of sleep before our father's cardiac arrest?

"Should you decide to keep him on life support, your father will not have a very meaningful life. He will not be able to eat, breathe or stand on his own ever again. He is in pain. We don't know if or when he is going to wake up. If he does, he will be in a vegetative state."

But millions of Canadians are living meaningless, empty lives. Should we kill them off too? I thought. All this man needed was a yes, from my brother, from my sisters, from my mother or from me; one yes and he could clear his bed for the next patient, we would clear the hospital quiet room for the next family.

"In situations like this you have to think of what he would want, not what you need. For some people, the ability to hear is enough for them because it keeps the idea of their loved ones alive. But this is selfish. What would he want?"

"Why would we give up on someone who never gave up on us?" whispered my brother.

How could we convince this man of how special my father is/was/can be? What was the right tense to use for someone in a coma? What if the doctor knew that even when we did not have a lot of money, my father would spend his last few dollars buying us all Kit Kats? What if he knew that my father did a silly dance to make us smile? What if he could see how much my father loved my mother and how much my mother loved him? What could we have said to prove to this man, to Canada, to Allah, that my father was worth saving? That he still had a life to live, weddings to plan, grandchildren to play with? But all this man saw was the X-ray of a destroyed brain stem, a protocol and a patient.

"If he has another cardiac arrest, infection or stroke, we will not revive him."

As if it was up to him to revive him, to give him life again. Who did this man think he was? Who speaks like this? I was convinced that this was my fault—for all the prayers I had missed, for all the times I neglected my parents, for all the moments I chose to be ungrateful. Maybe the faith we had all clung to since our beginnings in Pakistan was not real enough or was too far away. Maybe we had mispronounced a dua. Maybe Allah knew that I was a fairweather Muslim. Fear mixed with stories and languages not our own, on death, on the meaning of life, of science, suffocated each faculty of judgement, from the senses, to the emotions, to the intellect. Our bodies were tired, our minds were stuffed by Dr. Healey's diagnosis, but something within all of us remained untouched. In retrospect, when I tell this story I know now what moved us through that difficult moment: aqeedah, the miracle of conviction. We felt something that Dr. Healey could never measure or hear with his stethoscope.

In the profound mundanity of a hospital quiet room, I witnessed my mother give birth to my father.

"Dr. Healey, we are not like other families. We are Muslim. Where we are from, you take care of your own no matter what. We will not pull the plug. We will visit him every day. We will share with him our joys and tell him how our days were. He is still here with us, I know it. He will make a full recovery, inshaAllah. We are in full code."

My siblings and I did not know what this meant; we just knew that this was what we needed to say to keep our father alive, to keep him breathing. How my mother carried herself in that room impressed upon my heart a truth I will never, ever forget. The same courage with which she gave us all life filled up that room like a determined tide fills an empty shore, taking with it the years of feeling ashamed: of my mother tongue, the colours of our clothes, the scents of our food. For the first time in my life, I *saw* my mother in all her fiercely unapologetic presence, and I claimed her as my own, as a distinct marker between us and them.

One by one, we left that hospital room and made our way toward the intensive care unit to visit my father. I found myself learning the difference between saying dekhna and milna, the difference between going to *see* someone and going to *visit*. In that subtle linguistic distinction lay my father's existence as a human you meet with, not an object you look at.

There he was, lying on an elevated hospital bed in a coma, on life support, fitting Dr. Healey's image of him. The ventilator's oxygen mask swallowed his entire face; there were tubes everywhere: collecting pee, collecting feces, giving him water, pulling out blood. What had they done to my father? He was as lifeless as the objects that surrounded him. Where did my father go? Was he still in there? I could not understand what had happened to the man inside. Half of his face was covered with shingles—an infection he had contracted at the hospital. In Islam we are taught to say a prayer when we lose someone or something: We surely belong to Allah and to Him we shall return. It was then I learned what it meant to be mortal, to be truly vulnerable and naked.

I found myself stumbling over Arabic, Urdu and English to say to Allah that we had lost something about my father, but I refused to believe that we had lost him; something in my heart told me he was still there. No language, no dialect can form a prayer that can bring someone back from the finality of death.

Holding his motionless hand, I timidly whispered, "Assalamulaikum, Abu Jaan. All the other patients here are jealous of you. You are totally the most beautiful person in the ICU. Don't even stress about finances, Ami Jaan is running the business like a man!"

Ashamed of the insincerity in my tone, I closed my eyes and whispered, "Remember when you told me that the eagle does not fret harsh winds because they only help her soar higher? Well, Allah has given you another blessing in disguise, Abu Jaan. This is only going to help you fly higher. I promise you are going to be okay. We need you to wake up. Please wake—"

Before I finished the sentence, his index finger and thumb lightly pinched my sister's hand. I asked my father to hold her hand again, and his hand twitched again. With quickening heart palpitations and knots in my stomach, I rushed down the hallway to find a white coat, any white coat. Beaming with a desperate strain of joy, I grabbed Dr. Healey's arms and said to him, "He moved his hands! He is still in there, Doctor! He moves his hands when we ask him to!"

"Please do not touch me. Those are myoclonic jerks—knee-jerk responses to his environment that happen even when I turn the lights on or snap my fingers, a very bad sign which reveals how extreme the brain injury is. I think it is best if you do not overstimulate him."

Input, output.

But I was his daughter, not a snapping sound. The response he gave must have had more significance. Discouraged, disheartened and disenchanted, I found my way back to his room to witness my mother in another moment of strength.

"Munawar, I have never asked you to prove or show your love for me, but I am desperately asking you now. Please wake up or give us a sign." His hands and feet twitched. My mother's blood pressure spiked in excitement; she was on the verge of fainting.

But, Ami Jaan, they are myoclonic jerks, it is nothing, I told her. She did not care. She continued to repeat Surah Rehman and Ayat Al Kareema loudly—rhythmically chanting for the next few hours. Though my mother's voice was shaking, the strength with which she surrendered to Allah was comforting. My mother's strength came from a place not known by doctors, it was outside the grasp of the real. And from that place, she was rewriting our story and taking power out of the stories that gave Dr. Healey his white coat. At least someone was praying the right way, maybe Allah will hear her, I thought.

Though my mother taught me how to read the Quran, how to pray and how to be a Muslim, it was in this moment, with her most courageous act of love and faith, that she taught me what it meant to be a Muslim. That was when my mom shared with me the power of Ayat Al Kareema, how Hazrat Yunus read it again and again when he was trapped inside the belly of a whale; in this darkness, he sought forgiveness for his ingratitude and disbelief. But there is a twist. If pronounced wrongly its powerful effects can backfire and the reverse of what you are wishing for can happen. She also said that there were people in this world who purposely mispronounced it as a form of black magic to wish ill on others. Because of the possibility of such a fatal backfire, I held my tongue. At first I did not feel worthy to hold its truth on my tongue, but as my convictions grew stronger, as I moved beyond the blinding lights of scientific rationality, I came to inhale Ayat Al Kareema in every breath. That was the first and only night we left our father alone in the hospital.

That night I fell asleep clutching an old picture of my father I had taken from an old photo album from the basement. I whispered Abu Jaan again and again. I set out to materialize everything that was inside of me, my prayers, into the realm of appearances, in hopes he could see it from another dimension. That was the plan. In the picture, he was holding me as a baby and wearing his favourite maroon plaid sweater, the one he brought from the UK in the eighties. I had always wanted to inherit that sweater when he got tired of it. Was he still who he was in that picture? Did he predict this when he decided we should immigrate to Canada after his own struggle to find adequate healthcare for his own father in Pakistan?

Continuously whispering Abu Jaan, wanting to be heard, I thought that maybe if I projected enough pain into the physical realm, his spirit or energy would find me and give me a sign. So, I cried and cried and cried. He hadn't visited my dreams yet like he had with the others. Maybe I did not show enough sorrow to make a connection with his spirit. I had read online somewhere that during near-death experiences, spirits can leave their bodies through astral projection. If my father was in the house that night, I wanted to make sure he saw how much pain we were in and inspire him to wake up. It was to no avail; more pain failed to be the answer. Crying was not going to help me. The world did not need more pain. So I prayed, Ayat al Kareema, again and again. I ended up falling asleep to the sound of my mother praying to the Kabba through a phone call with an auntie in Saudia Arabia.

Doctors had given up on my father. To them he was dead—just another statistic to add to their collection of numbers. South Asian male, stroke, fifty-one years old. There had to be more to this world than what was inside those four white walls. How else did my father survive? They say that upon entry into this world, Allah has pre-determined certain dates, our wedding date(s), our birth date and the date of our death; however, with a sincere prayer from the heart, even the date we are meant to die can be changed. For my father to continue existing, there had to be more to this world than science. There just had to be.

I felt something in the ICU room; we all did. It was the same comforting sentiment we had felt when he was alive. It was his energy signature. There was a warmth in his hands I cannot use words to describe. Science told us that he was more in the *was* stage than he was in the *is*. But the way we felt in the room was as if his energy or presence was still with us. Not on a physical level, but in another dimension defined by spirit. If we pulled the plug, would his spiritual presence depart with his body? That night I had to accept the possibility of another dimension of existence to keep hope alive—to keep my father alive. He was in the leather jacket I was wearing. He was in my sister's smile. He was in my hands when I used them to donate money to the hospital. He was here with us—in the here and now. He was in the way my mother stood up for herself against all the white coats.

The next morning, my mother told everyone that she had many vivid dreams that long night. One in which my father told her that he could hear everything we were saying to him and that he was going to be okay. My sister spoke of a dream of him walking out of the hospital.

The next four days passed with daily hospital visits, family meetings with the doctors, consultations with specialists, lawyers and the media—but my father was still in a coma.

Although my family saw more and more jerks, and even a few tears here and there, the science of it all was that the new CT scan results made the likelihood of a miracle recovery even less possible. The four walls were winning. Some people remain in comas for months, some for years and others just never wake up. Forums on the Internet said his tears showed signs of consciousness. Dr. Healey said that because of the brain injury, the brain could no longer control the activity of tear ducts.

On the fifth day of his coma, my family and I walked into the hospital to see an imam and a priest offering a prayer for my father. Who were these men? The imam told them he was from the local masjid, where my father used to perform the Friday prayer. He raised his hands in the air to make a dua, and my family followed. He recited Surah Ar-Rehman, the beauty of the Quran, like a serene and soothing lullaby. My nanoo had once told me that this prayer was particularly effective in having prayers heard in a short period of time. The kindness of this random stranger stirred within me the kind of faith I was raised with, the one I lived in Lahore. A tiny droplet of water settled at the corner of my father's eye. A few misfired blinks later, his eyelids began to open. Like a phoenix arising from its ashes, like a baby calf being born, like a newborn waking up after his first sleep; finally, my father peered through his heavy lids. And just like that, Allah gave us back our beloved Abu Jaan, and changed life as we knew it.

A warm energy, the kind that emits when new life is introduced to this world, connected us. Our father had two birthdays to celebrate now. But what about what Dr. Healey had said in those four walls? My father was not supposed to survive. But he had. Now what? My family and I were now in the realm of the unknown—where *most likelys* and *probablys* were not good enough. In this realm there was no $1 + 1 = 2$—just X—boundless, indefinable and immeasurable. There were entities in this realm that could not be experienced through the five senses. My father's spirit, the spirits of those who had passed,

Allah, energies—everything outside had devoured the four walls. Another dimension had been added to my reality.

But science's disenchanting presence was not far away. Dr. Healey informed us that his opening of the eyes was meaningless, unless our father had the ability to track with them. Did he recognize us? Could he see us? Eye movement was science's way of indicating higher intelligence. But what about that warm energy we felt when he opened his eyes or his tears fell?

Everything Dr. Healey had to say about our father's conditions was moot now. The doctors had declared him one in a million. In emerging from the belly of the whale, it was clear that my father was given life again. But his future remained unknown, in this beautiful space indefinable by the language of numbers and probability. Within days of opening his eyes, he learned to track and respond to questions with nods. The doctors said he would never speak again. Two months after waking up, after having his tracheotomy corked, he released a hearty Alhamdulillah. Though his voice was soft, raspy and at times inaudible, he had defied the doctors' predictions once again. He did not need to learn English again. Though his short-term memory was at times dodgy and he experienced panic whenever he woke up, his long-term memory remained unharmed from the brain injury. Life re-entered his body bit by bit—first through his fingertips to his arms and then from his toes to his torso. No part of him had been completely paralyzed. Four months after waking up from the coma, with an army of occupational therapists, my beautiful siblings, my courageous mother and a walker, he took his first steps. At the end of that first year, after the New Year's countdown, as he was lying in a hospital bed in Brampton Civic Hospital, I will never forget what my father said: "For the first time in my life, I am beginning a new year with absolutely no fear."

Everything was out of the ordinary now. Three years from one hospital to the other, and the only night my mother left him alone was that first night. My mother stayed every night there, prayed without end, as my siblings shared shifts to cover the time she was running the family business. Where we all got the strength to continue moving, living, breathing in that difficult time is beyond us. It's been almost four years now and we are happy, my father is living a meaningful life, learning to eat again, walk again, and my mother is as strong as ever. There are difficult days, difficult months, but the convictions that found us despite the many layers of darkness will remain with us always as endless sources of resilience, of home and of courage. The greatest miracle was not my father's recovery, but Allah's mercy. From the prayers of the Sikh Punjabi woman who helped my mother call for help in that first critical moment, to the priest whose name we will never know, to the imam who we never saw at the masjid, to the endless prayers from family, friends and angels near and far, this is how you read stories from the Quran, with your heart, and emerge from the belly of the whale. And since that fateful moment, I keep Ayat al Kareema on my tongue, and the truth of Allah in my heart, wherever I go, for when you witness a miracle, it is very difficult to go back to just surviving.

Canada is My Land

Siddiqa Sadiq (Pakistan, Saudi Arabia)

I am thirty-six years old, and I have lived in Canada for twenty-two of them.

Before immigrating, I resided in the desert peninsula of the Kings of Arabia, commonly known as Saudi Arabia. It is much like Canada, which is also a land of immigrants. At one time or another, everyone has immigrated to Canada, and the immigrants now more or less rule over the Indigenous minority. Similarly, in Saudi Arabia, you run into more non-Saudis than native Saudis; as in Canada, the Indigenous people have become the visible minority. However, unlike in Canada, the native Saudis hold the keys to all the ruling powers of the country.

I was a visible minority there, as I am here.

I was born in Pakistan, but I have never lived there. I can't communicate for more than a few minutes in any of the Pakistani languages without substituting an English word in there. Nor do I entirely relate to most Pakistani customs.

In Canada, I have had people question my origin so many times. Pointing to the centre of their forehead and asking me why I don't have a dot there. Twirling their hand around the top of their head and asking: "Do all men have to wear a turban?" These are Indian customs and, having a Pakistani background, I cannot answer such questions. Furthermore, I am as Canadian as any other Canadian. I go tobogganing, cheer for my local NHL team, make sure I take any visitor for poutine, do a regular Tim Hortons run, visit the sugar shack at the end of winter to get the best maple syrup and above all feel goosebumps when singing our national anthem. Yet the first question I am asked almost every single time I meet someone is where I come from.

It gets more comical when I have people slow down their speech to speak with me. Using unpretentious vocabulary and adding tags to their rhetoric. Enunciating each syllable and pausing after each adjective. Hand signals, borderline sign language, add to the entertainment. Shaking their hand vigorously when saying: "Be careful, the coffee may be hot!" Shrugging their shoulders and slightly shivering when commenting on the weather: "It's really cold, isn't it?!"

The other day I was reading a book titled *Communication Skills for English as a Second Language* on the bus. A Caucasian man, unquestionably Canadian, sitting next to me kept looking over. The gentleman asked if I was learning much from the book. I looked over at him and before I could answer, he offered me a good deal on English courses, flexible class times, online lesson options and above all, the first hour of my classes for free!

"I will have to look at my work schedule and get back to you," I replied.

"Where do you work, if you don't mind me asking?" he asked.

"I am an English teacher," I said.

Border Crossings

A Day in the Life of the Many Me's

NikNaz K. (Iran)

LinkedIn alerts me to congratulate a former colleague on her appointment to the Diversity Lead of the company we used to work for.

"How times have changed," I think. Two decades earlier, at that very company, I had to speak vaguely about my personal life to avoid outing myself. Being out was not an option. Being a woman of colour in the competitive field of IT consulting was as much of a corporate rebel as one could get. Now everywhere you look, organizations are jumping on the diversity bandwagon, creating diversity initiatives to publicly announce their commitment to their minority staff. There is now a National Centre for Diversity and Inclusion, people can become certified diversity professionals and an annual award ceremony for Canada's Best Diversity Employers just celebrated its tenth anniversary. That doesn't mean all companies participate equally. The commitment of many does not extend beyond tokenism; they check off the diversity requirement after appointing a staff member or two to lead diversity in the organization—ideally staff who meet multiple minority criteria. At the other end of the spectrum, there are those that have embraced the complexity and tensions of intersectional identities and are committed to systemic change. By the time I left the company in 2008, I used to joke that I would make the perfect poster child for diversity, checking off at least three minority status items. Perhaps if I had stayed, LinkedIn would be sending messages to my network to congratulate me for some role or other in the diversity portfolio. But here I was, being told by LinkedIn to congratulate my former colleague. Could I bring myself to?

I remember the last day we interacted—the events that unfolded over the day and the conversation where she posed her question, rhetorical or spiteful, I'm still not sure which. But I can still feel the shock of that affront and how it happened at the end of one of my many long travel days across the border.

At that time I travelled for work regularly and had to cross the US border on a weekly basis. I was fairly accustomed to the gaze of people trying to peg me as either a man or a woman. I would notice their quizzical looks as they stared at me, hoping to find a gender identifier to grab onto. If they were with someone, the self-generated puzzle would be accompanied with a few quietly exchanged words: "Well he walks like a man," the first one would whisper. Staring at my hips, the other one would say: "Maybe, or a boyish woman?" Not convinced, the first would offer an alternative perspective: "Perhaps a gay boy?" And then almost in unison they would stare at my chest to see if they could find another clue. There were also the many attempts at figuring out my nationality, real nationality, as I was too dark to be a real Canadian.

I was born in the Middle East, in a country where one of its recent presidents claimed that there was no such thing as homosexuality there. Oddly, those were my thoughts when I was growing up in Iran. I felt different and alone in my difference, and all the social cues suggested that it was in my best interest to keep those differences to myself. With no access to words or a social support structure to help me understand and unpack my feelings, finally, on a hot summer night in July 1996, I left Iran with hopes of a better life in Canada.

Years later, by the time I started climbing up the corporate ladder, I knew I was more than just an Iranian-Canadian. While the hyphen offers me the flexibility to introduce the different aspects of my identity, in its linear simplification and compartmentalization, it fails to recognize the tension and transformation within each dimension. I reside in the hyphen between Iranian and Canadian. I identify with neither and both, live each separately and together. I further complicate the hyphen as a Queer-Iranian-Canadian. Queer resonates the most, but in and of itself is not sufficient. It is similar to my sense of identification as a woman—without queer, woman on its own does not paint an accurate picture. I am that in between space that disrupts, expands and challenges the boundaries of Iranian, Canadian, queer and woman. Over the years I have made many attempts to live each identity distinctly but have gradually learned to hold the tension among them and live them all in their rich messy complexity.

On that particular travel day ten years ago, after the yellow cab dropped me off at the Vancouver airport, just like any other professional traveller—with a carry-on suitcase in tow and a laptop bag on top of it—I zigzagged through the amateur travellers and steered my way to Air Canada's self-serve check-in station. I followed the usual steps to check in but the computer system persistently refused to accept my identity. I double checked my itinerary, repeated each letter and digit of my confirmation number out loud and then skimmed through the rest of the information. That's when I realized that my ticket had been issued for Mr. rather than Ms. It was the gender discrepancy between my passport and ticket that was throwing off the machine's binary logic. To proceed I needed the matter settled. What was I: man or woman? I stood in line to have one of the airline employees help clarify the matter. After the few people who were ahead of me had cleared the lineup, the airline employee looked up from the counter and said: "Sir, can I help you?"

When crossing the border, I am frequently "sirred" and am accustomed to letting it slide. But in this instance, the irony triggered a chuckle and as I walked up to the counter with a friendly grin, I half-jokingly said: "That is precisely the problem. I'm not a man. And I think that's the reason I can't check in using the machine." I continued to explain what had happened. Blushing red either with embarrassment or discomfort and without looking up from his monitor, the employee apologized for the inconvenience, asked for my passport and started clicking away on the keyboard to pull up my record.

After some digging around and speaking with a few of his colleagues, he figured that the reason for the confusion had most likely been due to a system update of the airline's rewards program. For members who had not specified their sex and salutation on their record, the system had made the best guess based on their name. Apparently Niknaz has a male edge to it and my record ended up with a Mr. as its salutation. He again apologized for the inconvenience, looking up briefly from his monitor to make some attempt at eye contact—probably something that he had been taught in a corporate training program—and said: "I can fix the problem for this reservation, but before you make any other reservation, you need to call the rewards program and confirm your ID." I cut him off: "What does that mean?" Clearing his throat, he mumbled: "You'll probably need to send them a copy of a valid ID that confirms your information." He then briskly proceeded to make the necessary corrections to my current reservation. Not wanting to make him feel any more uncomfortable, I didn't ask any further questions, but could feel the pangs of frustration forming a lump in my throat as I thought: "They made the mistake and I need to take the time and send them the legal docs that verify that I'm a woman. They don't even have the courtesy to take my word for that." Shortly after, with my boarding pass in hand, I was on my way to the immigration lineup, checked in as a woman.

When the immigration officer opened my passport and read "born in Iran," the privileges my Canadian passport granted me disappeared. It happens to me every time. After a series of questions, all in an attempt to reveal any possible threats I might pose, I am sent to the immigration office, where I sit behind a green door, waiting for my name to be called, my heart pounding.

Each time, the exchange is similar. I try a smile, a warm greeting, which most often falls flat against the cold gray countertops that are the only prominent features of the windowless room. I then resort to simple politeness and passive obedience to get through the interaction as smoothly and quickly as possible. The questions mostly revolve around my ties to Iran, why I am travelling to the United States, and my ties to Canada, but most importantly, why it is that I have a valid Iranian passport. As part of the process, each time my index fingers are digitized and I have a webcam moment. More questions; finally my passport is stamped and I can leave the immigration office area and go to security. There was that one time I was asked my marital status and when I responded "single," I was told: "No surprise, looking the way you do, who would wanna marry you." Taking a quick glance at the four big white American officers behind the counter, I was reminded who held the power in that dark, grey room and wisely chose silence as my response.

The process that day didn't take any longer or shorter, nor was it any more unpleasant than other weeks. Stepping out of the green doors, as I tried to find my way out of that area, a junior officer standing close to the exit looked at me and called out: "This way please, sir." I was only a few steps away from him when he must have realized his error and said: "Can I see your passport, ma'am." Already feeling drained from all the morning interactions, I gave my passport to him without saying a word. After flipping through the pages and finding what he was looking for, he handed it back and said: "Thank you, sir," and pointed to where I could exit the area.

Later that evening in a semi-fast-food restaurant in a strip mall in a small town in the Midwestern United States, I was delighted for the company of my Canadian colleague. At various times throughout the travel ordeals of my day, I had envisioned this time with her as a peaceful respite where I could finally let my guard down and relax, and that is precisely what I did. After all, I was in the good company of another perfect poster child for diversity.

While this was the first time we were sharing a meal together, we knew enough about each other to feel comfortable and for the conversation to flow. Out of respect for her more traditional Muslim practices, compared to my more forgiving spiritual beliefs, I had refrained from ordering an alcoholic drink and was content with my ginger ale and grilled chicken salad. We talked shop during dinner and it was only after we had both finished our meals that the conversation took a more personal turn. She shared a little about her marriage, her childhood and how her family had ended up immigrating to Canada. Comfortably sunk into the fake leather booth, feeling much respect for the courage and strength of this woman who sat in her wheelchair with her hair meticulously covered in a veil, I opened up about my day and the multiple layers of discrimination I had experienced that morning.

I can't remember how far I had gotten in my story when she interrupted and said: "Do you know that Islam bans homosexuality?

Nowhere in our religion are same-sex relationships acceptable. They are punishable by death."

This wasn't news to me, but I was taken by surprise and shocked at how quickly my peaceful respite had converted to another battleground. Still exhausted from the morning and the many interactions in which I had to defend aspects of my identity, I made a slight attempt to explain how there are different interpretations of the Text. But given my weak argument, she immediately objected and defiantly said: "There is only one interpretation." I assumed that interpretation was most likely the one she had chosen to believe and decided to let the conversation slide.

After that we must have gone back to our hotel together through the parking lot surrounded by outlet stores that had closed for the day and fast-food joints that were waiting for their last customers to leave. With my fate determined, we were back to talking about work, and it was only within those confines that our interaction continued.

Back at the hotel, I called my girlfriend. Her voice provided me the security blanket that I needed for the lump in my throat to finally burst. Hearing about my day, the irony did not escape her—to have my identity bashed at the beginning of the day because of my country of birth and my ties to Islam, and to have it bashed again at the end of the day because I was not a good Muslim. To the border officer, I'm a scary Muslim, to the Muslim, I'm an utter failure—regardless, I seem to be guilty.

Looking again at the LinkedIn post, I wonder what could have changed in my former colleague's life that she came to accept other interpretations of the Text. I would hate to think that she was promoted to the Diversity Lead still believing that I, and the likes of me, should be punished by death.

End of a Rainbow

Michelle Doege (United States)

We lounge on our rooftop patio; the sun warms us as it gets ready to set over the top of Turtle Mountain rock. We have been together twenty years this summer. Hard to believe until I notice Vindu's halo of white hair encircling her forehead, my formerly firm thighs now soft. Both of us just over fifty, we have travelled a world together, and we embody many countries inside our skins. Vindu is Indian but was born in Nigeria. I was born in Forest Lake, a small town in the heart of Minnesota. Vindu spent summers in Africa with her family and attended boarding schools in India. My entire life spanned two-hundred miles and two states, my longest journey to my grandparents' farm in Wisconsin across one state border. When old enough, both of us couldn't wait to leave home. I immediately left my small town, eager to open up and take in this wide world, and Vindu went to school in Singapore and then the US, where we eventually met and fell in love. Who would have guessed when laying eyes on each other on that frigid Minnesota morning that we would end up here—happily nestled together in British Columbia amidst this bursting sunset. Landing in Canada fifteen years ago, we were in search of a place to call home. We needed a country for our love.

June 26, 2001: Quetico, Canada

From Minneapolis, we rent a sturdy Subaru Outback to make sure we get across the northern border in time for Vindu to claim her permanent residency status. First step: One of us needs a legal foot in Canada so the other can try to follow. As we are a same-sex couple, India is not an option. America, the supposed "land of the free," does not allow same-sex marriage nor legal support for same-sex couples to immigrate. After six years, neither of us can stand the thought of being apart. At least if Vindu gets accepted into Canada, our worst-case scenario is a cross-border relationship—she in Windsor and I in Detroit.

We drive north through Minnesota to get to the border. So much is a blur in that time of transition. There are the immigration officers with their sharp-edged questions, the photos, the sound of that entry stamp: Ker-plunk! Vindu becomes a permanent resident of Canada. On the Canadian side of the border, it looks the same but tilted slightly in ways that are difficult to name. We drive along Rainy Lake—with its pristine waters and thick forests, a few fishing boats, and islands, yes, lots and lots of islands.

We camp at Quetico Provincial Park to celebrate Vindu's acceptance into Canada, and in some small and timid way, our new beginnings. On French Lake, we sit on the bottom of our canoe facing each other in a quiet bay, toasting with our wine and nibbling on the cheese plate between us. When we start to canoe back to our campsite, we are hit by a fierce and unexpected storm. Our life jackets tight, we paddle hard as water leaps into the canoe. We are not up for this, maybe not Canadian enough. We think our beginning in Canada just might be our end. Stroke after stroke. Harder and harder. Arms giving out. But we make it back to our tent. Vindu opens the zipper, stands in the triangle of the door like Zeus ready to take on the storm. Somehow feeling fierce, maybe fiercely Canadian, ready to face more storms to come.

July 1, 2001: Minneapolis

I was born on Canada Day, long before I knew such a day existed. Long before I knew such a country existed. My small world, my sense of family and home, was deeply woven into the Midwest until I graduated high school and was ready to bolt. Only then did my world open up beyond those small borders—to Colorado, to New Mexico, to falling in love with a woman from India. On Canada Day 2001, we post my immigration application, making a plea to the Canadian government to allow us to stay together:

> We [Bell, Unger & Morris] are requesting that the Visa Officer consider this application on humanitarian and compassionate grounds. Supporting documentation related to the bona fides of the relationship, the duration of the relationship and the hardship that would result if this couple were separated, are included as part of this package.

> Michelle: Vindu and I want and need to stay together. It would devastate us if this could not happen. We have built a strong life and love together over these past six years, and even though we have not been able to be legally married, in every sense of the word we consider ourselves married and family to each other. Canada, and your acceptance of same-sex couples, is the one chance that we have to remain together.

> Vindu: Michelle and I are a bi-national couple that do not share permanent residency in the same country. Falling in love and desiring to create a life together know no boundaries, but immigration legislation in most parts of the world makes it difficult for same-sex couples from two different nations to be together.

Rainbows span the globe—the two tips touching down in different countries—Indonesia and Thailand, Argentina and Latvia, the US and India. Many bi-national same-sex couples try to get one tip to touch down in their home countries, hoping they can crawl across that high arch and end up with their love in one place. We are not all refugees, our individual selves not necessarily threated by violence or persecution, but we are not merely immigrants either. We did not choose to migrate freely. We are binational same-sex couples who merely seek a country, a refuge, for our love.

Christmas 2001: Minneapolis

At the U-Haul dealer, a seventeen-foot truck with a flat-bed trailer waits for us in the lot, seems to call to our Honda Civic (who we affectionately call Sheba) to hop on. Just a few days before Christmas, I learn the intricate details of driving our car up the ramps, clamping the ramps down tight and locking several straps and bolts and gadgets to make sure Sheba doesn't bounce off. Seems important—I listen intently, look back and forth between the diagram and the trailer. I drive the whole rig to our apartment and park in front of the signs: "Do Not Park Here—Moving Truck Arrives Wednesday." My godchild and her brother and sister show up, my sister, my father later in the day to get the car strapped on safely. We put the big furniture in first—the couch, table and chairs, the bed and dresser. Boxes wheeled out on a dolly are hoisted up and stacked tightly to the ceiling. Vindu's bike goes in last. Mine will stay. We have to get Vindu across the border in the next forty-eight hours or she will lose her residency status. We will drive to Ottawa in this moving truck, and then I will head back to Minneapolis to teach one more semester at the university. Before we turn our wheels north on Boxing Day—whatever the heck that means—we have one last Christmas to celebrate with my family.

We are so caught up in Christmas that we don't notice the blizzard approaching. Tomorrow we leave for Canada; half our rainbow migration is complete. Home is Minnesota. Home is India. And yet we need this third country to stay together. We are grateful. We are sad. And I am angry. I am being forced to leave my home. What is it that defines our sense of place? Of home? It is in the details, I'm sure. The long, straight road driving through cornfields to reach my grandmother's hug at the door, the one-room schoolhouse on the right just before my grandparents' house. My childhood home surrounded by trees, a forest. I had no idea how much those oaks wrapped around my body. My mother's light laughter in the kitchen as she cooked. My dad's humble trailer in this trailer park, all of us stuffed inside. The smell of hot bread and ham. As always in my family, so much is left unsaid. We don't always know how to say. So we look at each other and then look away. Our minds and hearts left to toss about on the pillow later that night. When we are ready to leave Dad's trailer, to drive away from family, Dad peeks out between the dining room curtains as tears stream down our contorted cheeks. This same scene will happen, over and over again, each time we drive back to Canada over the next many years.

Early the next morning amidst a whirl of a blizzard, I shovel out our U-Haul. We must hit the road. We have sixteen hours to get Vindu across the border. The first turn of the wheels sends out a loud squeal, a haunting sound to start our journey. We feel numb. Chaotic, like the blizzard outside our window. A silent roar. We hardly speak, focus on the road. A road we often cannot see. We squint to try to see what's in front of our truck. All our belongings, our entire life packed into this long tube as we crawl through this frozen landscape of white. Only our cab, warm from the heat. We find relief from the blizzard through Chicago. A whiteout hits us hard again in Michigan. Vindu tries to drive; she can't, stops. In all this tension, we scream at each other—our howls trapped inside our cab, no one around to hear. We finally see the border. Creep up slowly. Are asked to pull over. The border patrol opens the back of the truck and looks in. Vindu hands them her paperwork—Ker-plunk!

New Year's 2002: Ottawa

We wake up from our rock-hard sleep at the Windsor Super 8 into the same bluster of white. We quickly throw on our clothes and scamper out the door for one more white-knuckle day on the road. Too tired, the tension somehow diffused on this side of the border. We sit mostly silent as we head to Ottawa. We miss our exit, drive right past. Now lost on unfamiliar streets, we scream at each other again. Finally, we turn our truck around and glance at our apartment building, a tall pillar of tiny lights jutting into the sky. We grab our keys from the front desk, open the door to our tiny one-bedroom. We're not crazy about it, but it doesn't matter—we have arrived. We blow up our air mattress—put it in the centre of the living room and then head back down to the parking lot to free Sheba. I can't wait to get behind her small wheel, to navigate these city streets, to go out and get some Chinese food and a much needed Tsingtao beer.

Hours later we wake up in our barren apartment, glance at the clock. We have six hours to unpack and get our truck back to the U-Haul dealer. We know no one in Ottawa to help us. We are on our own. We reserve the elevator with padded walls, pile up boxes and furniture outside the door, ride up and down the elevator all day long until we can't stuff one more thing into our tiny apartment. Twenty minutes to return our truck. We get lost on the way and have one more tense scream. It's good for us to have practical tasks: unpack dishes, position furniture, hang pictures, go to the grocery, stock the fridge, stuff the bathroom cabinet with toilet paper and shampoo. In just a few days, I will drive back to Minnesota for my last semester, my immigration application still stuck in the system. Vindu will stay in Ottawa, do her best to get us started in our new life. I'm sure we celebrated New Year's Eve, but neither of us has memories of that night. On January 2, we drive to Windsor. The next day, Vindu will hop a Greyhound back to Ottawa. I will drive on to Minneapolis with the passenger seat empty.

May 18, 2002: Between Worlds

On Victoria Day long weekend, I drive to Canada—our rainbow migration almost complete. I have been renting a room in a friend's house in Minneapolis, talking to Vindu on the phone as I stare out the window at a large oak tree. Vindu feels bone cold in her first Ottawa winter. We fight during most calls, so mostly decide not to talk. I am sad without her. But I am even sadder at the thought of leaving home—my family, friends, teaching, this familiar life I have built up around me over a lifetime. We hold off on me quitting my job, hoping Vindu will get a more permanent one before I quit. We're getting tired of being apart; we know the thread holding us together is wearing thin. The day I turn in my notice to the university, Vindu signs a six-month contract as an International Development Consultant. She will make more money in a day than either of us ever imagined. Yet, she is alone. She is depressed. Weight is melting off her bones, off her small frame. Each time I see her, she weighs less and less. Despite our best efforts, we are in danger of not making it. Our Lesbian and Gay Immigration Task Force support in Ottawa tells us most couples don't.

In the dark of morning, I drive out of Minnesota alone. I do not want to see anyone on this, my final goodbye. It is too much for my heart to hold. The rest of my clothes are packed into the back of Sheba along with a box of books, papers, a lamp poking up like a passenger, my bike tacked onto the back. Today, I will drive toward Vindu. She will take a Greyhound bus toward me. By the end of this day, we will be together in Windsor—all our belongings and each other—on the Canadian side of the border. I have no idea if we will make it, but we must try. I drive through Wisconsin with my heart heaving for all that is left behind, for all that is unbearably uncertain. I dream in a fog most of the way, listen to tunes to get me through the madness of Chicago. My heart pounds as I approach the Canadian border. With no formal papers, I'm afraid they won't let me through with a car packed full. My place in Canada is still uncertain. The guards ask a few sharp questions, then let me drive on through.

My body, now alert and tingling—I move slowly toward downtown Windsor, toward the bus depot. I catch a glimpse of Vindu perched on the side of a curb, now a thin brown woman, and my heart knocks against my ribs. Amidst all our fighting, I couldn't have imagined how good it would be to see her. I pull up alongside, leap out of the car and into her arms. We check into our usual Super 8, then head out for some Chinese food. Sitting across from her, there is no other place else in the world I want to be. My home is with Vindu, her home with me. We gaze into each other's eyes as we stab our chopsticks into some pretty horrible spicy beef.

2002–03: Ottawa

My immigration application is held hostage in the aftermath of September 11. Instead of looking for a job, I become "super wife," cruise three grocery stores in a week searching for all the sales. I cook, I clean, I make some pretty bizarre meals from all that bargain food. We give ourselves fifty dollars a month to spend on fun, which usually gives us a few rounds of hot dogs perched on a curb or a splurge on some pizza at the Westboro Beach. We are terrified of what it will take to get our feet on the ground in our new country. We lie awake most nights. In bed, we read some affirmations inspired by Shakti Gawain to help calm our nerves: "I am at peace. I have my right and perfect work." And then, enthusiastically and together: "We love and appreciate each other. Our life is abundant and fulfilling!" Ottawa is the most stunningly beautiful city either of us has ever lived in. On weekends, we hike the Gatineau Park and walk or bike along the Ottawa River. When feeling brave, we cross that river and try to navigate all that French. When the Queen comes for a visit, Ottawa goes into a frenzy of a celebration. We live right down the street from where her tiny feet will tread. I can't quite get my head around all the craze. The Queen of England—what?

December 3, 2002
Extended Visitor Visa (BB091 777 652)
Conditions:
1. Prohibited from engaging in employment in Canada.
2. Prohibited from attending any educational institution.
3. Must leave Canada by 28 June 2003.

Vindu wears a suit to work each day, marches into a marble and glass tower. She travels for work, sits in front of large microphones at the UN in New York or the Hague. She is doing the job she critiqued during her Masters and PhD—people in towers making fat paycheques off development work for the poor. We need the money. We need the stability to start our life in Canada. She is the only one who can work. I take a picture of her in a suit. She looks ridiculous. This Suit Vindu is not the woman I fell in love with, the one with a small backpack travelling to the villages or slums in India. My immigration application will be held up in a constipated system for almost two years. Our immigration lawyer calls to tell us my application did not make it through an important cut-off, that I must reapply for immigration, that I must start all over again. Tired of holding us up financially all on her own, Vindu sits down on the edge of our bed and weeps.

March 2003
Reapply for Canadian Immigration (File: B 042 899 975)

May 2003
Apply for Extended Visitor Visa
Receive FBI Police Clearance
Request RCMP Police Clearance
Complete Medical Exam
Pay $975 Landing Fee

July 2003
Letter to Ottawa MP—Plea to expedite application

September 2003
Medical Exam expired
New Medical Exam ordered

October 2003
Receive permanent residency papers in the mail
Drive to the US, then back into Canada—Ker-plunk!
Become a Landed Resident of Canada
Eat lunch at Tim Hortons with other average Canadians

I am white. I am American. I have Western degrees that transfer easily into Canada. I have close to perfect English. I have a job. My first job in Canada is to teach English to mostly recent immigrants at Algonquin College. Chinese doctors and Argentinian engineers squeeze into thirty-one tiny desks in five neat rows in front of me. They look at me eagerly—to teach them English, to help them make a life for themselves in Canada. With my white skin and fluent English, they assume I have been a good Canadian forever. Doctors whose credentials do not easily transfer to Canada want to become nurses. The Argentinian engineer seeks help in applying for a job teaching at the college. Because of his English, I know his chances are slim. Their journey looks long. So much longer than my own.

Once Vindu gets off work from the marble and glass tower, I pick her up and we go to evening French classes. It seems important that we know French. We tilt our heads at the Quebec licence plates: "Je me souviens." What the heck does that mean? To save money, I bring our dinner to eat in the car before class. We eat stir-fried cauliflower and rice out of Tupperware. Cauliflower was on sale at the farmers' market, so it is cauliflower soup, cauliflower salad and now this stir-fried cauliflower that is stinking up our car. Everyone in our French class has brown skin except me and the Quebecois teacher, who is often verging on drunk. Vindu and I are trying to add one language to our already fluent English. Everyone else in the room is learning English and French to add to their Arabic or Spanish. We sit next to an Iraqi couple. She has managed to get work in her area of computers; her doctor husband is a construction worker, wielding a hammer instead of a scalpel. We are an odd foursome—Muslim, lesbian, two of our countries on the verge of the Iraq War.

Everyone wonders why I immigrated to Canada. They are confused. Amidst their flowing hijabs and thick accents, I stumble, magically throw up smoke screens around my answers. They understand why Vindu is here, from India—of course she would come to Canada for a better life—but why me? Why do Vindu and I come to these French classes together each week? We are privileged, yes, and yet deep inside we are not. We too have left our countries and homes behind. We too are worried about making our way in Canada. We are like them, and we are not like them. We already had decent jobs. And yet we were forced to leave, to start all over again because of our love.

The Rainbow of No End

We are fortunate: There is a happy middle to our migrant story. Our decade in Ontario before we moved to BC was abundant—we landed good jobs, bought a solid and humble home, even got married in that home surrounded by close family and friends. We have also been fortunate to move to the Okanagan—to this land of big sky and rainbows—where our spirits feel most at home. Several of our close family have died over the past fifteen years, since our migration to Canada. I feel them in this wide sky. My father, grandparents, my aunt lingering somewhere out there. No heaven. Just their life energy dispersed into air. With the passing of time and loss of loved ones, my sense of home has shifted. I feel I belong to this wide sky beyond borders, instead of this earth where we draw lines into the soil. Not a sense of rootlessness, but more a belonging to something bigger.

Vindu and I have struggled; our rights have been violated—yes; but in the end, we have landed right here—together in our love. There are couples now, even as I type these words, that face persecution or violence in their country for being gay. Where it is illegal, or shunned, or simply difficult to live who they are in body and heart. Same-sex couples, falling in love across borders, searching for a home for their common throbbing heart.

The Pull of the Azores

ESMERALDA CABRAL (PORTUGAL)

On our first night on the island, I awoke at three in the morning. I got out of bed, stepped onto the balcony and looked out to the blackness of the ocean. The moon was full; its reflection lit a path to nowhere on the water's surface to my left. Straight ahead, dozens of lights dotted the expanse—the fishers were out in their boats. I wondered if they slept or worked at this time of night, and what they thought about when they were alone in the middle of the ocean like that.

The waves pummelled the beach, their frothy crests iridescent in the moonlight. A breeze blew the fine hairs on my arms. I grabbed the edges of my housecoat and crossed them tightly to my body to ward off the chill in the air.

Eric came up behind me and rested his hand on my shoulder. A big squeeze.

"It's beautiful here," he said. "Do you realize there's nothing between us and Antarctica except for those little boats out there?" He kissed my cheek. I took his arms, wrapped them around my waist and let my hands rest on his forearms.

"It feels so good to be here," I said. "I love how the air smells like the sea, that salty fishiness, and I love how the surf pounds the sand like that."

We only had one week on São Miguel this time. We had been back as a family before, a long time ago when Georgia was a baby and

Matt was a shy five-year-old. At the time, Matt openly flinched at all the cheek pinching, head patting and kissing every time we said hello or goodbye to someone.

"I'm not Portuguese, Mom," he told me when we were back home in Vancouver. "I don't like it there."

I remember feeling like his words had pierced my throat. My stomach tightened and my eyes blurred with tears. Eric noticed my reaction and tried to comfort me. "He's just a little guy; he doesn't know the impact of what he's saying," he said. "We'll try again another time."

So here we were, trying again, with our now teenaged children. Matt was a loyal fan of the Portuguese soccer team and Georgia couldn't remember being here before, but she had been looking forward to being on an island "in the middle of nowhere." Both had prepared themselves for all the inevitable kissing that would come with meeting my old friends, cousins and casual acquaintances.

The island of São Miguel is one of the nine islands of the Azores, strung across the mid-Atlantic between Lisbon and New York City. At sixty-five kilometres long and about eight kilometres wide, it is the largest island of this Portuguese archipelago. I left the island at the age of seven when my family immigrated to Canada, and yet, more than four decades later, I still catch myself referring to São Miguel as "home."

Why am I tied so strongly to a place I only lived in for a few years? Is home where you are born, no matter how short your time there? Is it where you live the longest? Is it where your children are born?

I have travelled to many countries all over the world, but the pull to visit the Azores is always there, lingering somewhere between my heart and my gut. Each time I return, my friends and I pick up our lives together as if no time has passed. Our friendship feels effortless.

This time, it had been more than a decade since I last visited. I was eager to get back to the island after such a long absence, but I was also apprehensive. In the last few years, I had grieved the back-to-back loss of my parents and I had been devastated by my sister's death from metastatic cancer. In São Miguel, Mário, my friend since I can remember, was killed in a cycling accident two years before. So much had changed and I was afraid of sinking into a sea of my own tears when I met my landscape again. Still, I figured the time was right to confront my sadness and try to make sense of the chaos of my grief. It was time to go back home again.

At breakfast the next morning, Georgia broke our jet-lag-induced silence by saying, "Do you think we can close the windows tonight? The waves were so loud last night I couldn't sleep."

I almost choked on my bread. The sound of the waves had always comforted me when I was a little girl, especially when I was trying to fall asleep. As an adult, I still feel a sense of calm come over me when I hear the rhythmic lapping of the ocean. I felt a twinge of disappointment at Georgia's question and decided not to address it, but to change the subject instead. Maybe if Georgia played in the ocean, she too would learn to love the sound of the waves.

"Well, let's go tackle those waves right now," I suggested.

The beach was across the street from our apartment, and to my surprise, Georgia ran onto the sand and right into the water. She loved the beach. The sand was dark and sparkly, and the waves were relentless. Georgia, Eric and I played in the water for hours while Matt sweltered on the sand. He would go in the water later, he said. He was waiting for just the right moment. Really? I couldn't believe it. I wondered if he was perhaps intimidated by the big waves, so I didn't push it.

The following day, we headed to the piscina, an area of natural swimming pools among the dark lava rocks that dominate the coastline, in the town of Lagoa. This was where I had learned to swim. I needed only to look over the low barrier past the ticket booth and I could almost see my father there in the kiddie pool, holding me under my belly when I was three or four years old, and swooshing me in large circles. "You're practically swimming," I'm sure he told me many times.

Some of the pools are the size of a large bathtub; others are fifty metres or more, with wide openings to the sea. While there aren't the daunting waves of the beach, the swell rushes through the openings, and at times it is an adventure to just get in the water. You have to time it right but in case you get it wrong, there are ropes to reach for and hang on to so as not to be carried away to the wider sea.

Matt loved the piscina. He and I chose the largest pool and we floated and swam and jumped off the rocks. Georgia would not get in the water. She wouldn't give a reason either. She found a flat rock and sat on her beach towel under an umbrella with knees to chest, sunglasses and a frown on her face.

"But you loved the water yesterday."

She shrugged and said, "I prefer the beach."

Later she told me she had found the bottomless water scary. At the beach, she could at least touch the bottom. And she remembered me telling a story about an octopus I had seen in one of the pools the last time I had been there.

I could accept my children's fears, but I also felt frustrated. I decided I would give up trying to please both of them at the same time.

Back at the apartment, after showers and naps, I asked about dinner. "How about rice and limpets?" I had seen a sign on a restaurant window by the piscina that said the special of the day was arroz com lapas.

Silence.

I love this dish. It's similar to the more common Spanish paella, but there is no meat, just seafood. This version, my favourite, is made with lapas, or limpets, a type of sea snail that has a conical, instead of coiled, shell and attaches itself to hard surfaces with a muscular foot. Limpets are common along the rocky shores of São Miguel and they are considered a delicacy in Portuguese cuisine. I not only savour the taste and chewy texture, I also like how each morsel transports me back to my childhood, when I would go to the seashore to pick them by the bucketful and eat them raw.

I grabbed my phone book and looked up my old friend Mário's brother, Dadim (his nickname), and dialed his number.

"Alô?"

"Have you started dinner yet? Want to go for arroz com lapas?"

"Madinha, is that you? Where are you?"

Madinha is my nickname. No one else uses it except my island friends.

"I'm here! Staying on the beach. Just got here a couple of days ago. What do you say, want to join us for dinner?"

"Oh my god, of course, I mean, yes … I mean, let me check with Dulce, yes, she's saying yes, let's go."

When I hung up the phone, Georgia said, "I can't believe you just did that, Mom. You just call somebody out of the blue like that? Someone you haven't seen in over ten years?"

"Yes. He's my friend," I said.

Dadim's mother lived next door to him, so I stopped in to see her while Eric and the kids went on to pick up our dinner guests. Senhora Eduarda had not only lost her son Mário two years before, she had lost her husband a few months later. He died when she was in the hospital getting her right leg and the toes on her left foot amputated. Poor circulation, she said.

I knocked, then let myself in. "Alô," I called and walked through the house.

She was sitting in an armchair in the sunroom, looking serene. She had been looking out the window into the back yard. She wore a black, short-sleeved dress with a string of pearls around her neck; her hair was coiffed perfectly. Did she know I was coming? No, Dadim told me later. He hadn't yet told her I was in town.

She looked at me, smiled and said, "It's been so long."

I bent down to greet her with a kiss. Beside her, on the side table, was a close-up picture of Mário sitting on a rock at the piscina—his hair was wet and tousled, and he was smiling. A gold chain hung around his neck. I bit my bottom lip to keep it from quivering.

She hugged me and caressed my hair, and I felt her tears against my cheek.

"How much life we've both lived since you were here last," she whispered in my ear.

"I'm so sorry. About Mário, about Senhor João, about your leg," I said.

"Our dead ones—they're in a good place. I believe that, don't you?"

She didn't wait for my answer. She continued, "I wish I could walk and feed my chickens. Sitting here all the time is boring, and I have too much time to think."

She was like family to me. My mother had been her teacher,

and she was my sister's godmother. Our families were intertwined through several generations.

She stretched out her arms, held my shoulders at arm's length and said, "Are those your mother's earrings you're wearing?"

"Yes! Yes, they are. I took them off her when she died and my father gave them to me. You remember them?"

"She wore those hoops all the time," she said.

She asked to see my family, so I walked across the driveway to where Eric, Matt and Georgia were picking cobs of corn with Dadim and Dulce in the garden.

"Hey, you guys," I called out. "Come on over. It's time for a few kisses."

No Country Calls My Name

ONJANA YAWNGHWE (THAILAND)

These are pictures of the exact moment the Chiang Mai to Bangkok train left the station in July 1985, from the vantage of the train car window: click, click, click. We are waving goodbye enthusiastically. The crumpled and wet faces of uncles and aunties we'd seen every day were growing smaller and smaller, framed by the window. Mae (Mom) was crying so hard, and even Por (Dad) seemed a little choked up, though he tried to joke through it. My brother was laughing, and I was clutching my plastic bag of snacks to my chest.

When Mae and Por told me and my brother Sawan we'd be moving to Canada, I had a vision of igloos and glaciers and frozen rivers. I was seven, and my brother was thirteen. They told me it would be cold, and I thought of whiteness and snow and mountains. But having been born and raised in hot and humid Thailand, I didn't know what cold was.

The plane trip seemed to last an instant. Somehow it seemed natural that we were thirty thousand feet above the earth, the ocean dark and glistening below. We arrived at midday, met by my aunt and uncle, who had sponsored us. I was disappointed not to see snow and was surprised that it was sunny and even warm. This was not the Canada I was promised. The light seemed too bright as the sun glinted off sidewalks and buildings. We had all dressed up for our first day: I wore a white blouse and blue-and-white checked bow tie; my brother wore a wool newsboy cap.

Our family is Shan, which are an ethnic group within Burma (Myanmar); Burma is filled with ethnic minorities like the Karen, Mon, Chin and Kachin, who live alongside the Burmese. Our people are from Shan State in the northeastern part of the country. The spoken language of the Shan is linguistically similar to Thai, but our written word is entirely different, full of circles and half-circles. For a time, the country was under colonial British rule, but it gained its independence after the Second World War. The British imported their language, style and customs to the country, and even today you can find some older folk in Burma speaking English with an impeccable British accent.

We first lived in a basement apartment near Vancouver General Hospital on the west side of Vancouver. We were told that the landlady was an elderly woman who wasn't used to kids, so (please!) we had to be very, very quiet. Because Mae started working at McDonald's and Por started working as a superintendent for an apartment building, Sawan and I were left alone all day since it was summer and school was out. We took being quiet seriously. We watched wrestling on the black and white television. We quietly listened to tapes of Carabao we'd brought over and sang "Made in Thailand" to ourselves. I would panic and hide every time the old woman upstairs would come down to say hello. The landlady would later say we were the quietest tenants she'd ever had.

We moved to a one-bedroom in Mount Pleasant, which at that time, was the neighbourhood where all the immigrants and poorer families flocked. Sawan and I shared a bunk bed placed in the corner of the living room, while Mae and Por took the bedroom. Mae started working as a cleaning lady. We kids went to school, neither of us knowing a lick of English except for the phrases "where is the toilet" and "thank you." The first day of school, I wore my prettiest yellow dress and copied the other students. When it became clear that I had no English, they had other teachers and students line up to try their language on me. I was the only Thai-born, Shan person in the whole school. But I saw white faces and Indigenous faces, and faces that resembled mine, so I felt sort of comforted.

English arrived quickly. To make us learn, Mae and Por forbade us to speak Shan or Thai. They forced me to read English books at home, even when I protested and cried. Eventually, my enemy, the English language, became my best friend and was the only thing that kept me company when I arrived home alone from school. My first novel was Roald Dahl's *The Witches*, but as I grew up, I turned to classics like Jane Austen, Charlotte Bronte, Louisa May Alcott and Lucy Maud Montgomery. I put away my Thai books. My mother tongue was lost, but I had found a newer, better mother.

When I was growing up, the question was always, "Where are you from?" which was a bad beginning because I knew whatever they thought, I was sure to disappoint. Somehow, people heard "Taiwan" when I'd said "Thailand." I wouldn't have dreamt of explaining about Burma and the Shan people. It was a conversation full of dead ends. Still, it was better than those clueless people who would automatically greet me with "konnichiwa" or "ni hao."

We never went on vacation as a family, and the only time I ever saw my parents relax and laugh was when old friends would come to visit. We'd finally go to a Chinese restaurant and the adults would stay up late drinking and telling stories. Visitors came from all over: Florida, Montreal, Thailand, England. We'd do the touristy things with them, like visiting Capilano Suspension Bridge, Stanley Park, Chinatown, Fort Langley. We'd moved to a two-bedroom by then, and from our bedroom my brother and I would catch snippets about my parents' lives in Burma and how they survived, how they lived in the jungles as guerrilla fighters, how my brother was even born there. Mae exclaimed, "That's why I never want to go camping!" These stories, however, were reserved for visitors only; these were never our bedtime stories and we were never told them. Mae and Por looked ahead for us, drilled into us the importance of school and getting good grades, of making our lives better. There was no room for the past in the bright worlds to come.

We didn't celebrate Christmas, Thanksgiving, Easter or anything else. We were Buddhists without a temple. The only glimpses of "Canadian" life were when my aunt and uncle would invite us for holiday dinners, and then we had turkey and ham, and Austrian stuff like schnitzel and apple strudel, because my uncle was from Graz (he liked to tell us he knew Arnold Schwarzenegger when he was a kid: "He was always at the gym!"). I actually didn't know what "Canadian"

culture was, since all of my friends were immigrants from the Philippines, Poland, Hong Kong and Vietnam. When I returned to school
after Christmas vacation, everyone always listed the presents they received, but it astonished me how many gifts other kids got, because
we just received one each. The tooth fairy confused me, and it never
occurred to me to believe in Santa Claus.

Of all the things we missed, it was our food we missed the most.
My mother yearned for green papaya, water spinach, chilies, fer-
mented pastes, rice noodles. She would substitute carrots for papaya
in our version of som tam. When people visited from Thailand, they
would bring us boxes of dried shrimp, soybean paste, shrimp chips,
dried milk and chilies, and in the kitchen we would get a direct reminder of home. Mae would drag us to Chinatown every weekend to
shop, feeling at home among the Asian faces, dried fish and the in-
comprehensible rise and fall of Cantonese and Mandarin. We rarely
went to restaurants; Mae was proud of her cooking skills. She prided
herself on making the cheapest and most mouth-watering meals. The
only thing was, she was unsure about cooking smells and made sure to
turn on all the fans and open the windows when she cooked.

What I learned in Canada was to be careful. I never looked at
anyone in the eye and barely spoke. My silence was my protector and
shield against the world. I came to look at my Thai girl self as rude,
loud and unspoken. She was selfish, demanding. My new Canadian-
ized self was timid, shy, hidden. But I excelled in school. Por was a
strict disciplinarian and angry; when we made a mistake, he would
force us to copy out lines like "I will be disciplined. I will not be stupid," over and over. He bore no questioning and would not listen to
our reasons. Sawan and I kept out of his way, like we kept away from
the drunks that were passed out in street corners and the women who
stood in the streets at night with very short skirts. We were in a new
world. We were unsafe.

It was also difficult growing up Asian and female. I was acutely
aware of how people saw me: did they think I was the brainy nerd?
A hyper-sexualized and willing sexual conquest? A dull, uninter-
esting robot? An innocent China doll? My biggest fear was that
I would be boring. I tried to become unexpected. After I saw the
movie *A Room with a View,* I pretended to be the very Edwardian

Lucy Honeychurch and spoke with a British accent at home. I got into the films of Krzysztof Kieślowski and became obsessed with foreign cinema; I took French and Russian. I learned tarot by heart and interpreted my friends' futures, all partly because I believed that this wasn't what your typical Asian girl would do. But the problem was that all the people I looked up to during that time were white, and the people I watched on TV and in movies all had white faces. I simply wasn't aware of all the possibilities I could be as an Asian girl. I was trapped in the mirror of other people's perceptions, that long corridor of reflections.

∞∞∞

It was only when I became an adult and I started reading other books—my dad's memoirs, a book about my grandmother—that I fully learned where we came from. Before Burma became a British colony, the land was under feudal rule, with different regions ruled by a saopha (prince). During the Second World War, the country was briefly under Japanese occupation, and after the war, the country was made independent.

My grandfather, Sao Shwe Thaike, was the last saopha of Yawng-hwe, and he became Burma's first president after independence in 1948. My grandmother became a Member of Parliament. But everything changed one night on March 2, 1962.

Everyone was sleeping in the house that night when a noise woke up Myee, my seventeen-year-old uncle. Fearing there might be an intruder in the house, he decided to go outside to investigate, dragging with him a ceremonial sword that was hanging on a wall. Suddenly, gunshots rang out. The rest of the family woke up and ran to hide in my grandfather's study, crouched behind a pile of thick Buddhist books as bullets ricocheted through the house. The sounds were sharp and deafening. When the bullets finally died down, my father and grandfather ventured outside and discovered the body of my uncle Myee. He had been shot. There had been a military coup, and my grandfather was arrested. Burmese independence was over. Months later, my grandfather would die in prison at the age of sixty-eight; rumour has it that his prison food was regularly mixed with bits of broken glass.

That night was the end and it was the beginning for our family. The night would stay with my father and the family forever: the page turned, the world overturned. My father went underground to join the Shan State Army to fight against the military regime, and years later my mother ran away to join him. He, my mother and my infant brother would escape to Thailand and try to live a normal life with fake identity papers. My father worked at a bank and my mother worked in a tourist office. They had built a castle in a storybook in which we played and imagined. They earned enough money in Thailand to design and build their own house in the middle of Chiang Mai, and were able to put us in private schools. But in the late 1970s, assassins on a motorcycle tried to shoot my father; troubles from the old country had followed. My parents were afraid, and my father's family (most of whom had immigrated to Canada at this point) urged them to come over. We arrived in Canada with everything we owned in a few suitcases and boxes.

Our family history casts a long shadow. Por got angry so easily and was frustrated at being a superintendent of our building, and Mae worked all the time. We didn't have much money. Our apartment was furnished with the dressers, mattresses, cushions and chairs that people left behind when they moved out of their apartments. We were allowed one new pair of shoes a year. I made Barbie furniture from empty cigarette boxes and their houses from plastic milk crates. The struggling people of Burma, the silent protests, the spilled blood, were placed behind locked doors. In Canada, the past had no sway. Every day, my father cleaned up the debris of lives leftover in the apartment building he worked in; every day, my mother rubbed clean the residue of lives, making it all new again.

∞∞∞

Every couple of years I get a shock. Like last time—I was walking through a busy food court in a downtown mall on my lunch break. "Chink!" I looked up in shock. It came from a most unexpected source, an older woman with white hair who quickly walked past me as she said the word. I felt like I'd been flattened by a bomb. I didn't know what had hit me or what happened. I didn't have time to react, and I just stood there in disbelief.

Thankfully, this overt racism doesn't occur very often, which actually makes it have even more of an impact, as it happens seemingly out of the blue. I've had people yell from cars, throw snowballs at me. Each time it happens, I'm not prepared: I feel a rush of anger, frustration at not having reacted, and most of all an inexplicable shame, as if I have done something wrong, as if there is something wrong with me. It's a reminder of my difference, but also a reminder that I let my guard down: *you let it happen again, you fool.*

There is a fierce loneliness in having both feet in two different worlds and cultures. You are estranged from the country of your birth and the country of your ancestors and can never know them; no land calls to you, not even in sleep. Call it the anteroom, or a kind of purgatory, or a liminal space, but the fact that I had no community to call home, that I belonged neither with the Thai, Burmese, Shan nor Canadians, instilled in me a fierce loneliness that has taken decades to be comfortable with. I accept that I am alone, just as I accept that the heart pumps blood to organs, limbs and to the tips of the fingers.

The discomfort of being born somewhere and being raised elsewhere is unique in people who've immigrated when they were children; on one hand, you retain memories of the land of your birth—the feel of the sun, the sounds of crickets, the sharp sour of a slice of green mango—but those memories are far away enough to come to you like dreams. On the other hand, there's the land to which you've arrived, a colder place, a place that clings to you and forms you with its promise of opportunity. I have never understood how it feels to belong, to know that you have a seat at the table. To be at ease and not question: should I be here? Do I fit in? I live on an unsettled sea, adrift between continents, where no sirens call my name.

When I was twenty-five, I returned to Thailand for the first time in nearly twenty years; I had just finished a master's degree in English literature and wanted to somehow return to my place of birth. I spent six weeks exploring Thailand on my own, moving from town to town every few days by bus or train. I got lost constantly. My Thai was merely enough for transactional conversations ("How much is this?"); foreign travellers assumed I was a local, while locals sensed I was more farang than one of their own. I was disturbed at the scores of older Western men with their arms around Thai women more than half their ages, and annoyed at tourists who just talked about going "elephant trekking" up north. I had never felt so lonely. And strangely enough, I also never felt more Canadian, though I couldn't articulate what exactly that felt like. I missed Vancouver: I wanted to smell the pine trees, feel the cool air, see the mountains and be near an unwelcoming sharp sea. Perhaps it had to do with the moment in the airport when I was saying goodbye to my parents. I looked back from the gates and suddenly saw that they seemed so frail and fragile; it was as if I was seeing them for the first time. It became clear: they, who sacrificed the lives they wanted to have, were going to die one day.

As I grow older and witness my mother getting older, frail and twisted by arthritis, these questions of belonging do not really bother me as much as they did when I was a young woman. My father died at the age of sixty-five from a brain tumour, never having seen the little democratic steps that modern Burma (Myanmar) has taken over the past few years. He died in exile, never again having set foot onto the land of his birth. My mother has visited Burma a couple of times now, marvelling at the growth and how expensive the country has gotten. As for myself, I don't feel a compelling need to visit; if I ever do, it will be out of curiosity and without expectation. I live in Vancouver, near the sea, and on the rare times that I get a feeling akin to homesickness, I listen to the sea breathe as tides rise and retreat, and inhale the salt of the Pacific that connects here to home, home to here.

57%

JIANNA FANER (THE PHILIPPINES)

My dad participated in National Geographic's Genographic Project. He paid about a hundred dollars for the kit, which uncovered his ancestry and explained where he was from. "And they say you're almost always surprised by the results," my dad said excitedly, repeating this tidbit every time the subject of the project came up.

He made it very clear from the beginning that this was something he wanted to invest in. Neither my mom nor I protested. I think neither of us really saw what the big deal was.

"You won't have to do it," Dad explained to me, "because ours will be the same. But you," he looked at my mom, "would need to do your own."

My mom smiled complacently and half-shrugged. "No, I'm not interested in that kind of thing."

"You're not even *curious*?" Dad said, shaking his head, as if not being curious about one's ancestry was a betrayal of identity.

As I understood it, the process involved taking a cheek swab, which was "painless," according to the website. Then, the National Geographic scientists would mail back a fancy box with a pamphlet and a link to a website that would tell the story. In my dad's case, it would be the story of a man who lived in the Philippines all his life—at least, until making the move to Canada—who found out he's not actually from the Philippines.

ooooo

Recently, my partner, James, told me about an idea he had for a tattoo: a tulip, with its roots somewhere near his wrist and the flower moving up his arm. It would be orange, possibly.

The response to "I'm Canadian" is almost always, "No, but what's your actual ... *ethnicity?*"

James calls himself Dutch, and looking up at all six foot one inch of him, you wouldn't doubt it. I told him an orange tulip for a tattoo would be a great idea. If you ask him further, you'll find out his mom is "Canadian." Because he was born here, James is content to call himself Canadian as well.

But ... I don't know. I can't imagine James ever wanting a maple leaf or the Tim Hortons logo tattooed on his arm.

ooooo

I have met James's extended family a number of times. His closest relatives live on Vancouver Island, so they come for special occasions. His uncle, Hans, has thinning gray hair, smile lines, thin-rimmed glasses and a single earring. He often wears tight-fitting shirts. Conversations he's had with his nephew—at least, the ones I've overheard—have included topics such as which kind of barbell to use for bicep curls, and counting calories and macronutrients. I guess Uncle Hans is the cool uncle.

Uncle Hans's partner, Bernard, is more reserved, with a quiet but quick sense of humour. In the few instances we've met, I have never heard him raise his voice, which is low, collected and humbly intelligent, in contrast to Uncle Hans's loud laugh and outspokenness.

Last summer, the two of them came without James's cousins. We were sitting out on the deck for dinner, having what is traditional fare in James's household during the summer: fresh greens from the garden, some source of protein and probably applesauce. This was the second or third time I had met Uncle Hans and Bernard in a year and a half of dating James.

We were talking about the absences of floors in some buildings.

James's brother, who worked in a building in downtown Vancouver between school terms, was talking about the missing thirteenth floor in his office building.

Uncle Hans, sounding worldly and intelligent, commented on the arbitrariness of such superstitions. "I mean, think about East Asian cultures. The Chinese buildings usually don't have a *fourth* floor, because the number four is unlucky for them." He looked to me. "It is four, right? Do you know why that is?"

There was silence for just a second too long. I felt the heat rush to my cheeks as I realized why he was asking me. "I don't know, actually, because I'm not ... Chinese," I said awkwardly.

"Oh!" said Uncle Hans. "I'm sorry. You are ..."

"Filipino," I replied, trying not to be embarrassed or irritated or anything.

Can you imagine what would have happened if I had told him I was Canadian? Wouldn't that have been kind of funny? It's certainly the truth.

But then, why would it have been funny? I *am* Canadian. I am Canadian, too.

Somebody cracked a joke about all Asians looking the same, and James' mom, trying to ease the tension, said, "Yeah, because *we* all look *so* different."

Uncle Bernard, who was sitting near me, turned and said, in his quiet, relaxed voice: "You don't look Chinese at all." For some reason, I remember this being reassuring. *Phew.* My physical attributes—my unchangeable physical attributes—are not falsely representing my identity after all.

I smiled good-naturedly and shrugged like it was no big deal. "Well, actually, I was reading a book about the meanings of numbers, and I read that it's because the Chinese word for 'four' sounds the same as their word for 'death'."

Everyone chimed in: "Oh! That's interesting."

And in my memory, the moment moves on and we probably talk about other things, probably about lifting weights and big biceps and healthy wrists, and probably nobody else except James remembers this moment, and probably, when I fill out forms asking about my citizenship, I need an option to check off "Canadian, sort of."

Later that evening, James and I were in his room watching Netflix. In disbelief, I murmured, "I can't believe your uncle thought I was Chinese. I'm so surprised he just assumed that."

"Were you offended?" asked James.

"No!" I said immediately. "It's just weird! I'm used to people asking, but people don't usually just ... assume."

James turned to face me. "Seriously. You can tell me. Did that actually offend you?"

"No, no," I insisted, even though I think some part of me must have known it did. Still—I knew James would not hesitate to talk to his uncle about it if I had admitted I was offended, and I think a bigger part of me knew I wanted to avoid that kind of conversation.

"Are you sure?"

I nodded. "Yes."

"Okay," said James, turning his body back around. He relaxed. I, clearly, didn't.

∞∞∞

There's nothing wrong with being Chinese. There's nothing wrong with looking Chinese, whatever that means.

My dad will scoff at anyone who comments that a person "looks" Filipino—because that doesn't mean anything. He'll point out that he is darker-skinned but will say with complete certainty that his mother-in-law has skin as white as snow and "would pass for white." He'll point out that there are Filipinos with flat noses and there are Filipinos with long, skinny noses. He'll point out that there are tall Filipinos and short ones. It doesn't mean anything to say someone "looks Filipino."

I've been approached at the bus stop by strangers who are talking to me in rapid Korean. I've been told I look Vietnamese, Chinese, Malaysian, or—with a tone of surprise—"not Filipino, though. I wouldn't have expected it."

∞∞∞

When my dad received the Genographic Project's results from his painless cheek swab, he was delighted and surprised. The results were just as surprising as I was expecting them to be, which is to say they were not terribly surprising: I would have been more surprised if the results told my dad he was actually Native American or Northern European.

The infographic that National Geographic sent my dad told him he was one of 691,609 participants. The particular tidbit my dad still wonders at to this day is that he is 2.6 per cent Neanderthal.

He is (only) 35 per cent Southeast Asian; 2 per cent of him is Oceanian, 3 per cent of him is Mediterranean.

"But do you know where 57 per cent of my DNA is from?" he said to me eagerly. "Northeast Asia! China! We're *Chinese!*"

The Darkened Room

FERNANDA PONTE (PORTUGAL)

I was eight years old when my family emigrated from Portugal to Canada. My parents, my ten-year-old brother, my two-year-old sister and I arrived at Dorval Airport in Montreal in July 1959. There was no one to meet us, no one to help us read the English signs or show us how to read a map. With only addresses in hand, we took a taxi and a long train ride, finally arriving at our new home in Kingston, Ontario.

Difficulties and sacrifices were soon to be a part of our everyday life, and as sacrifices go, we children had our share over the years. When my parents eventually found work, my sister, Lidia, and I were often left alone. Our days were spent playing together using our imaginations, as there was no radio or television to pass the time. We played word games in order to learn English. It was hard to learn the language, but even harder to understand the culture and social order. No matter how I tried, I struggled to belong. I was not in Portugal and I was not in Canada. I felt alienated and separated from life.

Leaving two young girls alone must have been difficult for my parents, but they needed to work and there were no other options at that time. Those days were long and lonely for two children whose lives were encased in a small and gloomy room. I was put in charge of when the food was dispersed, essentially becoming "mama" to Lidia.

My brother rode the bus for half an hour every day with our

mama to make other people's beds, pick up their garbage and clean toilets. There was no pay for him. This was the family working harmoniously together for the single goal of owning a house in our newly adopted country. And all we needed to be reminded of the goal was to look at the small quarters we were living in. The winter months brought in a cold draft, and the summer months were intensely hot.

I always wondered why our parents moved to a land so far away. Back home, my mama was a schoolteacher, and my papa worked for an American oil company. I felt safe. I enjoyed my friends and my freedom to act like a child with no responsibilities. Now I was a caregiver to my little sister while the rest of the family went to work.

In 1961 we lived in an apartment in the back of an old house. It was dark due to the windows facing north. The small room we used as a bedroom for my sister, brother and me was also our sitting room, and it was the hottest and darkest room in the apartment. When mama left for work each day, she locked the windows and drew the heavy curtains in our room so no one could see in. I always locked the screen and heavy wooden door after her departure and was told to keep them locked until she or my papa arrived back home.

One day in the middle of July, Lidia and I chose sleeveless cotton tunic-style dresses, knowing it was going to be very hot. As the sun rose higher outside our apartment, the heat in the darkened room became increasingly oppressive. We tried to pass the time in our usual way, but the clock on the wall screamed at us. Each tick-tock in the silence of the room reminded us it would be many more hours before my mother and brother would return.

I sat down on the floor with my back against our double bed, drinking water I had drawn from the tap. Closing my eyes, I began recalling a few of the many faces that had been on-board the crowded plane when we travelled to Canada. Some of the Portuguese families on that flight were staying in Kingston and others were travelling on to other cities in the vast country. Were the children of these immigrant families left alone for long stretches of time? Did any of them feel as I felt? That we were losing our childhood? Or was it more like the personal sacrifices that all families must make, as papa had said several times at the supper table?

"I can't breathe and I feel so hot," whispered Lidia. "I feel tired and just want to sleep, Dee," she added, as she slumped against the end of the bed.

"Don't move. I will be back," I said, walking over to the kitchen. I picked up a towel, wet it with cold water and placed it over Lidia's head. The water dripped onto her face and down her neck. Her cotton dress with yellow ducks hand embroidered along the hem and collar became plastered onto her skin. My own dress felt damp. Our mama was gifted with creative hands, and she made most of our clothes. She had brought bits of beautiful fabrics from Portugal and enjoyed making simple dresses with unique decorations on them. Though I longed to have a store-bought dress just once, I felt quite grateful for Mama's cool and practical design. The water continued to run down Lidia's face and onto her dress. But I could see it was not enough. Lidia told me again that she couldn't breathe and was very hot.

"Dee," she whispered, interrupting my thoughts.

"Yes," I answered, looking at her worried face.

"Why doesn't Mama stay with us? Why do we have to stay alone? Did they leave us alone back home?" she said in a very soft voice.

I gathered my sister into my arms, holding her, and quietly told her, "They have to work in order to buy us our home. It will have a large garden for us to play in." But as I continued soothing her, I considered her question: No. We were never left alone in Portugal. We had family to look after us when our parents went to work.

I helped Lidia remove her dress and wet slip, leaving her with her panties. I removed my dress too, leaving my slip on out of modesty, since I was the oldest. It was still getting hotter. I looked toward the door and heard my mama's rules: "Do not open the door at any cost, for you don't know who will be on the other side that could harm you both. Keep away from the windows and keep the drapes drawn closed so no one sees in. No one is to know that you are here alone."

Today the rules were becoming harder for me to keep.

"Are you feeling cooler?" I asked.

The lack of air and intense heat were clearly making it difficult for her to respond, so Lidia simply nodded yes. And then I saw her eyes pool and a single tear ran down her tiny cheek. Lidia communicated with her eyes, so I knew she was frightened. "Are we going to die?" she asked.

"No, we are not."

"Are you sure?"

"I am sure we are not going to die," I assured, brushing my tears with the back of my trembling hand. "Let's play a game." I wanted to distract her.

"Okay, Dee," she murmured.

"Lay down, Lidia, and close your eyes. We are lying on the cool grass under a perfect blue sky. See the fluffy clouds sailing by? What do you see in them? Do you see a dog, a kitty cat or maybe a funny rabbit hopping about?"

Lidia was silent.

"Think how cool you feel right now, okay?"

"Um, yes," she replied quietly, "I feel the difference. I feel cooler and I can breathe a lot better." But I could tell from her hesitation that she was unsure how she really felt and that she was just telling me what I wanted to hear.

As my Lidia continued to lie on the hard wooden floor, I kept hearing in my head what Mama had said about keeping the door locked. I began to worry that my parents would arrive too late to save us.

"Fernanda, take care of your sister ... a nossa pequena menina."

Yes, Mama, I will look after our little girl. I am listening to you, Mama, but deep in my heart I know I have to disobey you.

The conflict worsened in my head as I battled with the sin of disobeying. My mama had placed her trust in me to keep the door locked, and as of yet I had not disappointed her. But today, today was a test. Surely God wouldn't condemn me for trying to save our lives.

"Please, God, carry this burden for me, because I can't see any way out unless I break your commandments. God help me and show me what to do." I prayed on my knees.

Lidia lay on the floor with her little head cradled on a thin pillow. As I heard her gasp for air and saw her eyes brimming with tears, I suddenly knew what I had to do.

Getting up, I quickly unlocked the heavy door, swinging it open and raising the storm-door screen. Air started to flow. But it was not enough. I pulled back the heavy drapes, and grasping the handle, I opened the window, letting in a gush of fresh air.

I moved Lidia closer to the door, hoping the air coming through would revive her. Clambering over her, I went back to the kitchen and brought another wet towel, placing it on her head. She murmured a faint thank you and leaned against me.

I took a deep breath of fresh air and rested against the door-frame, hoping I had done the right thing.

Resting our heads upon one another, overpowered with fatigue and relief, my sister and I finally fell asleep.

That is how our mama and my brother found us. Crumpled together in each other's arms on the bare floor of our dark little apartment.

Mama began screaming on the other side of the locked storm door, "Meu Deus! Meu Deus! Minha queridas filhas! Fernanda, Lidia, my beloved daughters! Acorda! Acorda minhas queridas filhas! Meu Deus! Wake up! Wake up my beloved daughters! My God!"

Thinking the worst, she tried in desperation to open the storm door. When it did not budge, she banged on it hysterically.

"Abra a porta! Abra a porta, minhas queridas!" she continued, yelling and tugging at the door. "Meu Deus ajuda-me! My God, help me."

Startled by the banging and loud cries, I woke up and quickly unlocked the screen door, thinking my mama must be furious with me for disobeying. But she gathered me and Lidia into her arms, crying out loud, "Queridas. Minhas lindas meninas." She was kissing our heads, faces and anywhere her lips landed, pleading our forgiveness, crushing us in her loving arms.

Our brother's face was ashen. Staring, he said nothing.

I knew in that moment that I had made the correct decision and thanked God for guiding me.

As I was tucked into bed late that night, the question in my mind was, "What happens tomorrow?"

I could still hear my parents in their bedroom, Mama's muffled cries and my papa's soothing words of comfort. I looked over to my sleeping brother and sister.

"What happens tomorrow?" I asked myself again. But I knew that today I had grown in strength and wisdom, and that those two things would keep me safe.

When I look back at all the sacrifices my family and other families had to make while adapting to our new surroundings, I realize that in spite of the challenges we faced, somehow we became stronger, bonding together our old traditions and the new ones we made along the way.

Strata

Jasmine Frances Sealy (Barbados)

He tells me I smell like breath, not bad breath or good breath or baby's breath or a breath of fresh air, just breath in its primordial muskiness. We are dancing together, but not really, because he is on the floor spinning in semicircles on his back, his knees pulled up to his chest like a yogi tripping on ecstasy, which is more or less what he is. The party has begun to thin out around me. People dig their way through piles of damp boots and coats and stumble out into the icy blackness of St. Denis. Each time the door is opened, a small gust of wind blows into the apartment, sobering me up. I begin to turn in small circles, moving faster and faster. The party blurs before my eyes, a carnival of milky limbs and black clothing. I stop spinning and collapse onto a sunken sofa. As the room comes into focus and the white blur divides itself into slightly more distinguishable white bodies, I think I should see if any of these white people have some cocaine.

The breakdancing yogi on drugs has joined me on the couch. His hand is on the back of my neck, his fingers tugging on the tight curls found there, and all I can think about is how difficult they will be to detangle when he is through. He tells me I smell like breath and I ask him what he means and he smiles because he has thought a lot about this and he knows it is a good line. He says I smell like beginnings. Not beginnings like Monday mornings or sunrises, but absolute beginnings like the collapsing mass of planets and moons that are subsumed by a birthing star. He says I smell like black holes and dark matter. Like something older than life itself. I say it is probably just coconut oil. He is ridiculous and I know it. He has already cast me for a specific role in in the theatre of his single, white male existence. I am a tick on a list, a thumbtack on a world map, for him. But the attention of white boys is an unwieldy thing and I carry it like a box of mementos from a past I ought to forget. There was a time when women like me used their fair skin as a weapon, as a shield, the touch of a master in tenderness a means of avoiding the fields. I wonder what I am trying to escape. I wonder why his touch feels like survival to me. When he leans in to kiss me, I let him.

The air is caustically cold. The thin fabric of my holey leggings offers little resistance to the wind, but I wore them anyway because I long to be at ease with winter the way the others are. The street is silent but for the sound of his voice. He is beautiful in that white boy way, coatless in the December air, his shoulder blades slicing through the black of his T-shirt. I long for the inside of a taxi but he wants to walk, so I feign enthusiasm for the fresh air. He has a theory, something about the Internet and how we are generating a whole online universe of factually inaccurate information. False biographies and made-up historical accounts and too many quotes wrongly attributed to Einstein and Marilyn Monroe. He says this wrong information is becoming so vast that in the future, in thousands of years, when Internet anthropologists dig through the archeological remains of our digital worlds, they will have a hard time sifting through all of this inauthenticity. I say maybe the truest thing about our present is its ambiguity, its slipperiness, its propensity for duplicity. My teeth are chattering and my voice is unconvincing, even to me. I say I do not know the truth of who I am and even if I did, would the evidence of me—the Facebook status updates, the tweets, the selfies—would those bits of me that survive into the future, only to be unearthed by some graduate researcher in the year 3000, would they show who I really was? And besides, what is more real, the things people actually say and do or the so-very-human desire to mold the world, to make it fit our needs, to crop it and filter it and add a misquoted caption?

He is not impressed. He says it is not about me anyway. It is not about any one person, obviously. He says in the future we will all be lumped together as one past, one dead civilization. We will no longer be individuals. Assumptions will be extrapolated to all of our contemporaries based on the discovery of even a few digital remains. One YouTube clip will be worth a thousand words. I say those anthropologists are going to think we were really obsessed with videos of cats. He does not laugh at that. He is having a moment. He says when astronauts look down on Earth from their spaceships, they see one mass, one floating orb, but here on Earth we are too close up to the mirror, too myopic. We cannot imagine ourselves as one singular civilization castaway on an island in the sky. I say Greenland is an island and did he know that? But he refuses to be plucked from the ether of his existential reverie.

I realize then, as we traverse through the vacuous and milky darkness of Montreal at 5:00 a.m., that I could never love him. This boy whose individuality is so presumed, so innate, that he can only fathom its loss in some distant, abstract future. The same boy who told me once, in a drunken moment of rare and honest crassness, that he does not normally fuck black girls but he would make an exception for me or Rihanna. I do not have to imagine the loss of my individuality; I have always been a token to these people. I know that once this night is through, he will draw conclusions about every black girl he meets now, based on the things I say and do. He will lord his insider knowledge over his less-experimental friends at dinner parties. I will become an extrapolation, a piece of anecdotal evidence. I was born a fossil.

I sleep with him anyway. The sex is perfunctory and brief. Afterwards I sit on his tiny balcony that overlooks Parc Avenue. Two stories below me, the garbage is being collected, overpowering the scent of sesame bagels toasting in the twenty-four-hour Jewish bakery down the street. Through the large glass windows of the YMCA I can see spandex-clad bodies running on the spot, ponytails bouncing rhythmically. I think for the hundredth time of how much I love this city and of how desperately I long to escape it. I think of Canada in all its vastness and of how, despite the diminutive size of my island home, I never felt so trapped there. I worry about these Canadians with all their land, all that open space. With their easy smiles and open arms and their goddamn Tim Hortons commercials and their stolen inuksuk. Welcome, weary travellers, dive into our melting pot. I think maybe it is not so easy to be ourselves here as they made us believe it would be. I think of how wrong he is too, about the astronauts. I think they are likely just like us, peering out into the abyss, searching for something familiar.

The Weight of Loss

ABEER YUSUF (MALAYSIA)

One of my saddest moments came last year when I was in the bathroom of my one-bedroom apartment in East Vancouver. I looked around at the light-brown, marble-effect tiles, and for the life of me struggled to remember what the tiles of my bathroom in Malaysia looked like.

I thought hard—was it light-blue triangles? Was it pink offset with grey? I blanked.

Within minutes, I was in tears. I'd spent roughly twenty years of my life growing up in the same house, same room and same bathroom in Malaysia—and now, after three years in Canada, I'd forgotten something that was so familiar and close to my everyday life?

When it comes time to discuss immigration, the rhetoric in public record and popular culture always celebrates the new-ness of everything. The tone is one of unbridled joy and a narrative of conviviality—"Welcome to Canada! A better life and new beginnings!" the papers shout.

Yet no one talks about loss.

How you lose your language.
How you lose your places.
How you lose your memories.

None of this happens overnight. For the first little while, your hands and movements take time adjusting—still faithful to where your old light switch was, still obedient to the little acts you've performed blindly growing up elsewhere. You dream in multiple languages, with dialogue that is most likely peppered in code-switching and colour. Dreams with new hopes and aspirations of what seems like a benevolent system. You take in your new geography and surroundings, immensely excited and hoping, wishing, you could share this with all your friends and family who haven't seen your new life here.

Then reality hits. You experience a snide comment while walking past someone, a long stare from someone on the bus who looks your outfit up and down.

A little bit of your confidence and a bit of your energy is zapped, but you move on. Maybe they were just admiring your new coat, but forgot to smile.

Of course, the biggest irony about loss is that you don't realize that it's happened. You put up with all the challenges migrants face. You are told that your documents are incomplete and that you need to fill out more forms, which you have to attain from your home country. You find out that your qualifications are not recognized in Canada and you need to start over. You are advised to spend more time studying for that exam you thought you were ready to take. You are told that your English isn't good enough, even though you speak the language fluently and only your accent betrays you.

Time goes by and you gain skills that make you a better candidate to become Canadian. You blend in—what an achievement.

You're sitting in an Indian restaurant, eating your native food, and you see a raisin. You want to tell your friends a really cute story about what you used to call raisins while growing up. You can't. You don't remember what raisins are called in your language anymore. You spend the next little while frantically asking your friends what it's called, but they can't recall either—it's *your* language you can't remember, not theirs.

You travel back to the land that was once home, and suddenly your body betrays you—when did the light switch move? You don't remember the bathroom being quite so small and stuffy. When did all these things become so old? Your body tries to readjust to a home it knew so well, but suddenly forgot. It takes time for your body to memorize this all over again.

Armed with nostalgia, you go to the places you could swear you had memorized—that particular hangout spot, the restaurant or space where you spent eons in conversations with your friends about the most inane developments in your life. It looks different. It's not there.

In just a minute, your world changes. The physical loss of a space, a place, means you lose everything that goes with it. The place where you fell down, badly scraped your knee, and your parents made a huge fuss about you. The place where you exchanged numbers with your first love. The place you sat and stared at the world go by. It's all gone—and all you're left with is a ringing sense of longing, loss and nostalgia. The worst part?

You can never return.

This is the way it is, and this is the way it will always be. You will try to protect your memories, take mental and physical snapshots to make sure you can safeguard these memories from disappearing, but you'll fail.

You come back to Canada—with a burden this time, the weight of loss. You long for home, and a sudden homesickness overcomes you. Not just to go back and to spend more time with your loved ones, but an aching and longing that never leaves, and now rests uncomfortably but stoically at the back of your mind. Was it the right decision to come here? What will change the next time you go back?

Life goes on. You readjust and try to move on. You lose memories, but you also lose the opportunity to make memories. Your best friend's getting married, and after all these years of you two scheming and dreaming of the perfect man together, she'll get married without you by her side. Canada came in between the promise you made to be her bridesmaid come hell or high water—the distance, the amount it would cost you to fly back, the fact that you get fourteen days for a holiday but it takes you three to just get there—it all gets in the way. You see her pictures, silently and wistfully wishing you were there to see all these memories being made. Now you've experienced another kind of loss.

Each time you return to Canada after sojourns back where you came from, you feel further fragmented. This foreign place, this land you thought you could never belong to, where some people reminded you that you couldn't belong to, suddenly feels familiar, smells comfortable and begins to feel like a second skin that is easy to put on. What kind of a cruel joke is it then that as you fly back on the plane from the place you called home all these years, you land in Canada—which you now feel is home—and just one small moment makes you realize you can even lose a sense of home.

The migrant experience is shaped by being neither here nor there. You don't realize it, but your feet are constantly stuck: one in a country where you're uncomfortably and sorely trying to gain footing, and one in a country where you don't want to lose your home or stumble into a loss you can never retrieve.

I recently returned from a holiday in India, where I was born. My parents bought a house in Bombay ages ago, in an old colonial-style apartment complex when I was ten. Every year we'd go to the same house in Bombay, unpack, vacation for a month, pack up and then return to Malaysia, where my parents and I have been based for the better part of the last twenty years.

There's a beautiful tradition in India wherein when you get married, your entire house—be it an apartment complex, a bungalow, a mansion—your entire house gets lit up with fairy lights; it's an indication that a wedding is happening in the vicinity and that much happiness and joy is being exchanged and welcomed. Ever since I was a young girl, I've returned to my apartment complex year after year, imagining what the place would look like if I were to ever get married there—an indication of the happiness and new beginnings being ushered in and the celebrations taking place in our home. I always imagined this would be the house I would be married in, with a cacophony of chaos, bright activities and laughter taking place in the background.

This year when I went back to Bombay, my parents informed me that the house we lived in had to be sold due to creeping gentrification and the rapidly changing identity of our neighbourhood. I said my goodbyes to all my family members, and for the last time, to my home of sixteen years.

And just like that, I lost once more.

Authors

Ishita Aggarwal writes creative non-fiction, short stories and poetry and has had her work published in *The Soap Box*, *Brevity: Journal of Concise Literary Non-Fiction* and *Emerge Literary Journal*. In her spare time, she enjoys reading biographies, eating copious amounts of raw fish and daydreaming about her next vacation.

Nadine Bachan was born in Trinidad and raised in the suburbs of Toronto. She is a freelance editor and writer who currently lives in Vancouver. Her work has been published in *Hazlitt*, *Maisonneuve* and the *Best Canadian Essays* series.

Jamelie Bachaalani is an emerging writer from Edmonton, with a preference toward non-fiction. Her work focuses on adolescence, self-discovery and the human condition. When Jamelie isn't writing, she can be found trying to revive her beloved but forever dying cactus.

Josephine Boxwell is a freelance writer and media specialist. Since moving to Canada from the UK, she has lived in Ontario and British Columbia. Her short fiction and non-fiction works have appeared in several BC based publications, and she has a certificate in Creative Writing from the Humber School for Writers.

Esmeralda Cabral writes creative non-fiction. Her work has been published in various anthologies, *The Globe and Mail*, and aired on CBC Radio. She attended The Writer's Studio at Simon Fraser University and the Disquiet Literary Program in Lisbon, Portugal. She lives and writes in Vancouver, BC.

Michelle Doege is a writer, educator and engaged member of the literary community in Vernon, BC. A recent graduate of Augsburg's MFA in Creative Writing, she produced a collection of poetry entitled *Tonewood*, which explores ancestors and lineage and trees—and borders and boundaries—inside ourselves and in our world.

Jianna Faner is a grateful guest on Musqueam territory, currently studying English at the University of British Columbia and managing social media for Canadian Women in the Literary Arts. Like many Vancouverites, she loves figure skating, yoga pants and coffee, and like many Filipinos, she loves adobo, karaoke and her family.

Kasia Jaronczyk lives in Guelph, ON. Her debut short story collection, *Lemons,* will be published by Mansfield Press in spring 2017. Kasia has co-edited the anthology *Polish(ED): Poland rooted in Canadian fiction,* forthcoming in fall 2017 from Guernica Editions. Her poetry and short stories appeared in *The Bristol Prize Anthology 2016, The Prairie Journal, Room, Carousel Magazine, The Nashwaak Review* and *Postscripts to Darkness.* Her work placed first in the Eden Mills Contest in 2010, second in the GritLit Hamilton festival in 2015, and was longlisted for the CBC Radio Short Story contest in 2010.

Camila Justino is a Brazilian writer who has had four books published in Portuguese. She left Brazil in 2012 to live in Canada. She is currently studying creative writing at the School of Continuing Studies of University of Toronto and is writing her first novel in English. She lives in Toronto with her husband and son.

NikNaz K. Her tombstone will most likely read: She Made Things Happen. It will also say something about her strong sense of integrity and contagious enthusiasm. At heart, she relishes the process of creativity, whether it's painting new artwork or facilitating conversations to germinate a new organization. (NikNazK.com)

Nam (Namugenyi) Kiwanuka came to Canada with her family in the mid eighties following the Ugandan Civil War. She is a Canadian television personality and journalist. She was a VJ for MuchMusic from 1999 to 2003, and later she was host for NBA XL and CFL Crunch on Rogers Sportsnet. She was also the author of a popular column for the BBC's *Focus on Africa Magazine,* and in 2010 she directed a TV pilot that "celebrated the faces and places of Africa." In 2013 she was named an Emerging Filmmaker by the ReelWorld Film Festival. Nam is currently a host and producer for TVO.

Diana Manole, PhD, is a Romanian-Canadian poet, translator and scholar. She has published nine collections of poems, short fiction and plays, and contributed to numerous international literary magazines, anthologies, academic journals and collections of articles. (dianamanole.ca)

Miriam Matejova is a writer and researcher, currently pursuing a PhD in Political Science at the University of British Columbia in Vancouver. Her creative writing has appeared in *The Globe and Mail, Her Circle,* the *Inconsequential* and several travel magazines. She is one of the contributors to Caitlin Press' *This Place a Stranger: Canadian Women Travelling Alone,* and an editor of the *Project Nightingale* literary journal.

Sarah Munawar is a Muslim scholar and writer who is completing her PhD in Political Science at the University of British Columbia. Her family emigrated from Lahore, Pakistan, to Toronto, Canada in 1998 and are now living in Brampton, ON. She wrote *How to Emerge from the Belly of the Whale* as a testimony of miracle, in celebration of her father's resilience in the face of struggle.

Margaret Nowaczyk, MD, a clinical geneticist, is a professor at McMaster University. Her writing has appeared in *Geist, Examined Life Journal, Intima, Numero Cinq* and *Praire Fire.* She is a co-editor of a short story anthology from the Canadian-Polish diaspora (Guernica Editions 2017).

Kaija Pepper's criticism and essays on dance have appeared in *The Globe and Mail*, *The Walrus*, *Queen's Quarterly* and other publications. Dance Collection Danse published her trio of books on Vancouver dance history, and co-edited anthology *Renegade Bodies: Canadian Dance in the 1970s*. Kaija has been editor of *Dance International* magazine since 2013.

Fernanda Ponte immigrated to Canada from Portugal. She lives in Kingston, ON. Retired from the Royal Bank of Canada, she stays active through volunteering in her community. When her husband passed away in 2013, writing helped her cope with her grief. She is blessed to have the support of her family and friends.

Gina Roitman is the author of *Tell Me a Story, Tell Me the Truth* and *Midway to China and Beyond*. Her award-winning documentary film *My Mother, the Nazi Midwife and Me* chronicles her return to her birthplace—Passau, Germany, Hitler's home town. Her work has appeared in numerous anthologies and on CBC.

Siddiqa Sadiq is an English teacher. She lives with her husband and daughter in Chateauguay, PQ. She teaches in Old Montreal at BLI, an international-language school. When not working, she loves reading, writing and spending time with her daughter.

Aileen Santos lives in Acton, ON, with her partner, two children and two fur-babies. Her work has appeared in literary journals and magazines such as *ricepaper* and *Tayo Literary Magazine*. Her debut novel, *Someone Like You*, was published in spring 2016 by Two Wolves Press. She often writes about love, motherhood and issues of diaspora around belonging and connection.

Jasmine Sealy was born in the UK and raised on the island of Barbados. She is a graduate of the University of Toronto's International Development Studies program and the Writer's Studio at Simon Fraser University. In 2014 she was shortlisted for the CBC Quebec short story competition. Her work can be found in the Quebec Writer's Federation anthology of *New English Writing from Quebec* (2014) and the *Emerge Anthology* (2016).

Ayelet Tsabari was born in Israel to a large family of Yemeni descent. Her first book, *The Best Place on Earth* (Harper Collins) won the Sami Rohr Prize for Jewish Literature and the Edward Lewis Wallant Award. The book was a *New York Times Book Review Editors' Choice* and a *Kirkus Review* best book of 2016, and it has been published internationally to great acclaim. Her non-fiction has won a National Magazine Award and a Western Magazine Award. A graduate of the MFA program at Guelph University, she teaches creative writing at the University of Toronto's School of Continuing Studies.

Onjana Yawnghwe has been published in numerous anthologies and literary journals, and her first book of poetry, *Fragments, Desire*, is forthcoming with Oolichan Books. She works as a mental health nurse in Vancouver, BC.

Abeer Yusuf's life has been defined by living everywhere and nowhere. Being brought up between contrasts, Abeer has devoted her life to thinking about identity, race and belonging, and how we understand who we are based on how we move in the world. She enjoys puns, reading (especially illustrated children's books), balloons and the colour yellow.